Also by Eugene Fullerton:
Everyday's a New Day, 2009
Day To Day Secrets, 2009

The Older I Get,
The Wiser My Father Becomes.......

Eugene Fullerton

authorHOUSE®

AuthorHouse™
1663 Liberty Drive
Bloomington, IN 47403
www.authorhouse.com
Phone: 1-800-839-8640

First published by AuthorHouse 5/31/2011

ISBN: 978-1-4567-8109-5 (sc)
ISBN: 978-1-4567-8110-1 (e)

Printed in the United States of America

Any people depicted in stock imagery provided by Thinkstock are models, and such images are being used for illustrative purposes only. Certain stock imagery © Thinkstock.

This book is printed on acid-free paper.

To my parents, James and Theresa O'Neill Fullerton, who taught me how to love and to be the person that I am today, for the faith they passed on to me, and for the great gift they gave me……..
          "teaching me to work"

Introduction

I hope that you will enjoy reading this, my third book of poems, as much as I enjoyed writing them. This book contains a collection of poems, some written as far back as 1981, up to the present time. They cover a wide range of topics, some were written during the Troubles, some are words of wisdom and some were inspired by stories from my youth, but mostly they were spontaneous reactions to everyday life.

Seeing the finished article in print makes it all so worthwhile. When I say I enjoyed writing the poems, I would have to be honest and say that it was also a lot of hard work. The physical amount of time and effort putting it all together can be overwhelming and working with printers and checking word-for-word the writings is a very daunting task.

Eugene Fullerton.

Contents

Smoking

O Dearest Lord, upon my knees I pray to you this night
To take from me this habit, this terrible dirty plight.
Remove from me this awful crave, this burning aching pain
This thing, that rules my life, O Lord, and drives me near insane.

Dearest Lord, I know You'll help, I'm sure that You will care
Enough, oh Lord to listen, this burden I will share.
For though I'm not yet wakened, it haunts me to begin
Before two words are spoken – I once again gave in.

Dearest Lord, I've tried it once, I've tried a thousand ways
To kick this filthy habit, but yet, alas it stays.
So now into Your hands O Lord – some folks might think I'm joking,
But You're the only power on earth to help me stop this smoking.

EF, 1981.

Accidents

Is it any wonder there's accidents,
The way some people drive?
As sure as God's in Heaven how some of them stay alive,
For they never stop to think of cars, as little bits of tin,
Tacked together with some leather and a belt to strap you in.

Is it any wonder there's accidents
When people overtake?
It would make your heart stop beating
As you whisper "For God's sake!"
For they never stop to think that cars
Roll off assembly lines
And are only made to last a while,
To keep up with the times.

Is it any wonder there's accidents
When vehicles pass you by?
Buses, coaches, cars and lorries,
Every one of them fly.
For they never stop to think of tyres
Upon the wheels go round,
And could burst at any minute
And leave you on the ground.

Is it any wonder there are accidents
The way that cars are made?
Far too light and far too fast,
Any colour, make, or shade.
But there's one thing to remember
As you drive along in laughter
That it's better late here,
as early here after.

EF, 1986.

Song

I was walking down the street one day
When I looked upon the ground, and there he lay,
His face was old and wrinkled
His clothes were ten years old, his hair was grey.

I stopped to take a better look at an old man
As he sprawled there in the muck,
In his hand an empty bottle,
And I thought, "Now here's an old man out of luck".

Now we're rushing here and there and everywhere
And we're looking for an answer
To a problem that's as old as yesterday
Yet the truth is here and I must try to understand
'cause what I saw today is here to stay!

I turned to walk away when he called
At me and asked me for a hand
I leaned over him on bended knee and
He said, "Young man, you're kindest in the land".

"For many people pass this way and I know
that they've got lots of things to do,
And a broken down old beggarman has
Nothing here to offer them, you see".

Now we're rushing here and there and everywhere
And we're looking for an answer
To a problem that's as old as yesterday
Yet the truth is here and I must try to understand
'cause what I saw today is here to stay!

Well, I went my way but I said to him
As he lay there with his head pinned to the ground,
"Old man, you'll find the truth in life if you
Lift your head a while and look around,
For nothing in this life comes easy,

You won't find happiness unless you try,
But you're gonna have to get up and make a move
'cause if you don't, this life will have passed you by.

Now we're rushing here and there and everywhere
And we're looking for an answer
To a problem that's as old as yesterday
Yet the truth is here and I must try to understand
'cause what I saw today is here to stay!

EF 1987.

Time Out

O Lord, if we could only listen,
We'd truly know what we were missing,
Instead of plodding through the day,
We'd take the time to stop and pray,
And hear the words You have to say.

EF 1987.

Autumn

The Autumn leaves are lying on the ground,
With twisting, twirling movements they fall without a sound,
A selfless year of giving has come unto an end,
Their green and golden colours to us could only lend.

I look and watch them as they lie,
Upon the ground they wither and die,
The wind it rises, blows them away
And yet in abundance, most of them stay!
But brush them together, put them in a heap,
Leave them all Winter, your seeds they will reap.
Then look at the trees, transparent and cold,
No longer elegant, no longer bold,
But standing there naked without any clothes!

For they budded in Spring, they blossomed and bloomed,
Like shining knight armour their richness it boomed,
All over this country, all over this land,
When we are all gone, they still will stand grand.
For remember how hard we work and we toil,
That we're only here for a very short while.
We too like the leaves will wither and fade
And return to the home for which we were made,
For if man could in peace but only abide
And stand and watch the countryside
He would know in his heart, he would know in his head,
That everything possible has already been said.
For no matter what language humanity speaks,
And no matter what colour or creed,
To think that we're going to live here forever
Would surely be foolish indeed.

EF, 1988.

The Spider

I watched a spider on the wall,
How it could climb and then would fall,
I watched its legs, the way they gripped,
The way it moved, the way it slipped,
I watched it as it reached the top,
How it would stop and then would drop,
I watched it as it hit the floor,
And landed right beside the door,
I watched as it began to crawl,
The height of that tall slippery wall.

EF, 1988.

Fatty

I spy with my little eye
A little fat man eating Christmas pie,
His belly's round, his legs are plump,
Upon his back there is a hump.
His cheeks are flabby, his nose is flat,
His head is covered with a wee black hat,
The clothes he wears are far too small,
The buttons on his coat won't meet at all,
His trousers open, belt undone,
As he tucks into another cream bun.

EF 1988

Castle Ballroom

In Newry Street in Banbridge town,
A castle stands out tall,
Where people went there years ago,
To have themselves a ball.

Its brightly lit and shining front,
It stood out from the rest,
That's why they flocked from far and wide,
For it was the very best.

The bands they came from all the land,
They came there, big and small,
To entertain the many feet,
Who danced there in that hall.

I remember climbing up them stairs,
That took you to the floor,
The place was packed with patrons,
From the stage, down to the door.

The music that they played there,
Was crisp and loud and clear,
The girls just loved the well-dressed men,
Who came from far and near.

The ladies stood along one side,
The males faced them like bees,
And then they raced to pick their queens,
To the sound of The Lovely Lee's.

The timber floor bounced up and down,
The couples danced and sang,
They jived and waltzed the night away
In their ears the music rang.

And still we're together after twenty odd years
Since we met in that great hall,
For no matter how far you would travel by car,
The castle was the king of them all. E.F. 1988

Talk

Now there's talk of unemployment,
Sure it's always on the news,
Every day at every corner
People stand in ones and twos.
And there's talk about recession,
Factories closing every day.
Men and women on the dole queue,
Waiting for their unearned pay.
Now there's talk about the country
And the government's to blame.
Politicians sit uneasy, as they
Bow their heads in shame.
For they talked and promised all of us,
That they could lead the way.
Everyone went out and voted
And assured them they could stay.
But nothing's changed, it's still the same,
And no one wants to take the blame.
They just pass the buck to someone else,
While they hold on, to all the fame.

EF, 1989.

Life is a Race

Life is a race, as everyone knows,
The harder you run, the faster it goes.
The days are too short, they just disappear
The evening comes round, it would fill you with fear.
For you put your head down on the pillow at night,
Before you can blink, the dawn brings new light.
You jump out of bed, put your feet on the floor,
Pull on your clothes and out through the door.
Into the bathroom, face quickly wet,
Up to the kitchen, breakfast to get,
You gulp down the cornflakes, fast cup of tae.
You start a new day and you hope and you pray
And you try to help people in the things that you say.

EF, 1989.

One Drink Too Many

<u>Drinker:</u>
I had a drink last night,
It made me fight, a war went on within me!
I told 'yer man up at the bar to pour me out another jar.
And then I fumbled through my keys
To find the right one for the car.

"Hurry up, will 'ya! Have you that there poured?
My tongue is hanging out! Will 'ya get a move on!
I haven't got all night!"

<u>Barman:</u>
One, one, I thought, and that's it, I'm giving
That man no more!
I'll try and just persuade him to walk out
Through the door.
For the last night he was in here, just a few short hours ago
He fell and hit his head, an awful bang upon the floor.

I'll have one more barman, before I make it home.

EF, 1989.

Full

My belly is sore with fullness
A feeling I've often felt!
I've thought about it often
As on my knees I knelt!
I just never seem to stop eating
My mouth it goes up and down
That's why we so often visit
The shops in front of the town.

EF 1990.

Holiness

I once had a vision of holiness,
A lovely vision it was,
The place was surrounded with beauty
I couldn't believe my eyes.
I stood and I watched with amazement
To be sure of what I had seen,
And I lifted my head and I gazed,
The place it was spotless and clean.
To begin with, I thought I was dreaming,
So I stood around waiting for more,
And lucky I was for a moment
I was almost swept up off the floor.
Now I took a step back and I waited,
And all I could do was just stare,
For in the midst of the hustle and bustle,
I heard the loud whisper of prayer.

EF, 1990.

The Troubles

Two decades of trouble have taken its toll
Many innocent people struck from the roll,
Lives that are precious can never be bought
Can never be made, by the skills that we're taught.

The pumping of blood, the making of heart,
We here on earth wouldn't know where to start
Every movement of limb controlled by the brain,
Many people have tried but give up in vain.

And yet there are those who will never pay heed
But continue on down the dark road of greed,
Where money and power and evil prevail
They can't see a time when their actions will fail.

But God, in His glory, to them will reveal
His power and His grace, their hearts He will heal,
If only to Him they will turn and repent
For Jesus, His son, for us sinners, was sent.

EF 1989-1991.

Green Field

In a green field in Ireland in 1991
A shadow cast across it in the early morning sun,

The blades of grass were broken by the hammering of feet
As they pounded out across the earth, each other to greet.

A group of men were gathered up at each end of the land,
And two of them were playing a tune with pipes in hand,

The tunes were loud and noisy and each one told a tale
of bitterness and anger, as each were doomed to fail.

EF, 1991.

Ode to the Worker.

If you go out to the motorway
And stand in the early morn,
You'll see cars and vans and working men,
On the road since the crack of dawn.

Now they're heading off to the building sites
To start at eight o'clock,
All different types of tradesmen –
There's Joe and Jim and Jack.
And they come from all the different parts,
A tough and dying breed,
To share the talents in their hands
To meet the growing needs.

They're very little thought of,
At least in status terms,
But they can't be done without
In all the building firms.

EF 1991.

Businessman or Beggarman?

Businessman, or beggarman?
A question often asked,
And especially when the postman
Just seems to drive on past,
And even when he does stop
Our letterbox to fill,
It's only an advertisement, a postcard or a bill.
I wait for him each morning
Around the time of nine
To push the letters in the box
He's always there on time.
There are white ones with windows in,
Brown ones and pink ones, you name it,
But if I get a cheque this morning
I think I'll bloody frame it!

EF, 1991.

What is it?

"What is that thing up on the wall?" my daughter said to me,
"It's a football" said the little boy, looking up with glee,
"It's not indeed", the big one said, "Can't you see it's the moon",
"You're all wrong", said the oldest one, "Sure it's a saucer without a spoon".

Well I listened to all their comments, from the youngest one and all,
As to what this stupid object was, hanging from the wall.

"It must be the top of a chimney pot, that's fallen on its side",
"It's far to big, you silly girl, it's more like a revolving slide",
"It's nothing of the sort now", said the little boy again,
"Sure it must be an object for them to catch the rain".

Well I listened to all their comments, from the youngest one and all,
As to what this stupid object was, hanging from the wall.

"Well then", said my daughter to me, "Ach, Daddy, I know now,
The man next door has put it there, but I just don't know how!
My wee friend told me in school that she has got one too!"
And the wee boy said, "Without it, she couldn't watch TV!"

So I listened to all their comments, from the youngest one and all,
As to what this stupid object was, hanging on the wall.
And when they all, the three of them, said, "Oh Daddy, we wish ..."
I quickly snapped back at them, "NO satellite dish!"

EF, 1991.

Time Flies

Another day is nearly gone
Daylight begins to go,
Time to put my head down
It doesn't seem like sixteen hours
from I heard the rooster crow.

Another week is almost gone,
"It's Friday", says I,
It seems no time since Monday morn,
As the days just roll on by.

Another year is almost gone
The calendar says it all,
We stroke each day off with a 'tick'
And the 'tock' is on the wall.

Another decade passes by
As we struggle and we strive,
I seem to know more people dead
Than I ever knew alive!

EF, 1991.

Another song

Oh the night is nearly over
And a new day will begin,
How I long to see the morning
And to hear the sweet birds sing,
The sparrow and the robin
And the thrush with whistles sweet,
As I stretch my arms and waken
They're there, my day to greet.

Chorus.
Yet we're fussing and we're fighting
And there's war and strife around,
Everybody is complaining –
No contentment to be found.

Oh I long to see the morning
Another day that I've been spared,
And I thank the Lord above me
That "my prayers have all been heard".

EF, 1991.

The Poster

A little baby child is BORN , displayed up on the board,
Surrounded by its wombly blood, and umbilical cord.
It's caused an uproar in Belfast, everyone was shocked
It made the people turn their heads,
The whole damned place was rocked –

"Oh my God!" "Oh my oh my!"
"It's just disgusting", said a passer-by,

Holy God, I'm Just appalled
"Putting that up on a wall."

What do you think?

EF, 1991.

"For God's Sake"

I started work when I was young
My father kicked my ass,
He said I had to go to work
And I had to go to Mass.

I didn't always like the things
My father used to say,
"Would you wake up, son, for God's sake,
Away outside and play!"

And then when I'd be questioned
For things I hadn't done,
My sisters used to laugh at me,
'Twas them had all the fun.

"Where did you leave the hammer, son?
Were you foottering with that oul bike?
Sure I haven't a spanner about the house,
A never seen your like!"

EF, 1991.

A Tribute

I stood in the house where the man had died,
I listened and watched as his friends there sighed,
And I tried to see the sense and the logic of dying
As my eyes passed over his parents, who were crying.

I followed the hearse and the men that walked,
And I overheard as some of them talked,
"It's a bit late now", one dressed man said,
"To give time to our friend, after all he is dead".

And I sat in the Church and I heard the priest say,
That a good man from us had been taken away.
And he talked and he praised the poor man who had died
For the way he had lived and the way he had tried.

And I thought to myself as I sat in my seat
Of all the hundreds of people we meet,
And we wait to the day when they're all passed away
To give glory, give praise, a tribute to pay.

And I stood at the grave as they lowered him in,
His wife loudly sobbed and her face it was thin,
The young boy at her side, as he fought back the tears,
Will remember that day for many a year.

EF, 1992.

The Cattle-Grid

How many of you would know that a cattle-grid
Between two pillars placed,
Is pointing in no direction
No matter what way it's faced?
For the length's the same from end to end
In concrete it is cased
And the width it never varies
For the bars are equally spaced!

EF, 1992.

Thinking of You

When I was alone and thinking of you,
Trying to imagine the things that you do,
All of a sudden my mind would go blind
Memories of you I just couldn't find.

So then I'd sit down, with pen in my hand
And write of the days, of all we had planned
And try to recall the moments of love,
Shining from Heaven, a light from above.

EF, 1992.

Life

A man's life is very short
No matter what his years
Some day he has to leave this earth
And cast aside his fears.
For what is here is definite
A light before your eyes,
The moon, the stars, the rising sun,
They shine out from the skies.
For a man is born with nothing
But the skin upon his bones
The beginning and the end
He is very much alone,
For what lies beyond is uncertain
And faith he needs to have
For time it flies, it's just a blink,
From the cradle to the grave.

EF, 1992.

Pain

Unforgettable pain I witnessed as I watched
Slowly walking in sorrow, mothers and children attached.
Broken in heart and spirit, almost without hope
A future blinded without fathers to help them to cope.

Indescribable anguish weighed down on fallen faces
People out of favour it would seem from all God's graces
Unanswered questions pouring through each mind
Without consolation for those left behind.

Unforgivable actions carried out by troubled minds
The innocent left to remember the terrible times
Unity no more for them, taken away by men
Those without conscience or mercy to fulfil their gain.

EF, 1992.

*Written after watching one of Northern Irelands many, many funerals,
during the long history of troubles since 1969. All of us knew someone.*

Heaven

Have you ever thought of Heaven, the way that Jesus said?
Have you ever thought of Heaven, in your heart and in your head?
Some say that you'll find angels there,
Saints and sinners too,
Some say they are many, some say they are few.

Have you ever thought of Heaven, St Peter at the gate?
Have you ever thought of Heaven and arriving there too late?
Some say that He'll be waiting there
To open up the bar,
Some say the God has opened them
Already, they're ajar.

Have you ever thought of Heaven, the way some people do?
Have you ever thought of Heaven, is it false or is it true?
Some say that you'll find peace and joy
And treasure there beyond,
Some say you'll find relations
Of whom you once were fond.

Have you ever thought of Heaven, as a place to take a stroll?
Have you ever thought of Heaven as a place to rest your soul?
Some say God sent us Jesus,
The only Son he had,
Some say He came to save us,
And some say He was mad.

Have you ever thought of Heaven, when your life here's at an end?
Have you ever thought of Heaven as a place to start again?
Some say the road is open
Any time of day or night,
Some say it's everlasting,
A place of eternal light.

EF, 1992.

School Days, John 1958

Do you remember John, the day we started school?
My God, you looked like a fool,
In your wee short trousers and woolly hat,
Do you remember that John, do you remember that?

Boy, I'll never forget John, me and you
Heading down that footpath, faces blue,
Wee short coats and wellie boots,
Sure as heavens we couldn't give two hoots!

I'll always remember John, the very first day
Me and you we went round the back to play,
And you fell flat on your face in the muck,
You jumped up mad as a hatter and shouted, "Holy…. Lord!"

Do you remember John, the master with his knuckles on your head?
He said there was more brains in a half a stone of lead,
And he told the two of us, me and you,
To pull our socks up or we'd be in the stew.

Now the time went in John, and the days grew longer,
And me and you and school, we grew no fonder,
For the teacher and his cane and his big black cloak,
What we had to listen to, 'twas no joke.

But sometimes ah wish John I was back in school,
Sitting aside you on that wee stool,
With your wee short trousers and your woolly hat,
God I remember that John, ah remember that!

EF, 1993.

30

Thoughts.

I gazed down o'er the fields of green
The nicest land eyes ever seen,
My mind it wandered back in time
To things my father used to rhyme,
about life.

Life is short son, short and sweet,
There's hardly time for friends to meet,
So get your skates on while you can
And take a stroll across this land
And learn about life.

EF, 1993.

Seasons

As I wait for Summer time
It's not so far on down the line,
Winter's gone and spring is here
So Summer time is very near.
As I wait for longer days,
Is not so far away I pray,
Cold and rain go away
Warmer days are here to stay.

EF, 1993.

In Days of Old

In days of old when men were bold
Machinery not invented,

Men toiled with hands to work the lands
And struggled on contented,

They used their sweat the spuds to set
The corn and wheat to sow,

They worked behind the horses plough
And prayed that all would grow.

EF, 1994.

Three Score Years and Ten

Three score years and ten
Is the span for women and men.
The scripture readings remind us
Over and over again,
But I took no heed of this say'n
For then I was only ten.

Three score years and ten
Is the span for women and men.
The gospel message reminds us
Over and over again,
But then I thought I had plenty
For then I was only twenty.

Three score years and ten
Is the span for women and men.
Our departed ones remind us of this
Over and over again,
But then in my peak I was sturdy
For then I was only thirty.

Three score years and ten
Is the span for women and men.
The speed of the years remind us
Over and over again,
'Cause now I can't believe it's true
I've reached the age of forty-two.

EF, 1994.

Just Wash the Dishes

"Don't thank your Ma for the dinner,
just wash the dishes",
That for me, my children,
Would be my fondest wishes,
Do not burden her with work
That she does not deserve,
After all the time she takes
To make the meals and serve.

An empty plate it makes light work
And is grateful in its thanks,
Appreciate the prideful hands
For they rate high in the ranks,
Gather up the knives and forks,
The saucers and the plates,
It will help to please the both of us
If you all get on your skates.

There's a famous Chinese saying
'Many hands light work will make',
Try to put it into practice
Give your selves a little shake,
So then when the dinners over
You can all let go the tether,
Just get up and wash the dishes
Then we can all, relax together.

EF, December 1994.

War

The voice of a lonely woman
Echoes through our land,
The cry of a lonely child
Holding her by the hand,
The pain of a lonely people
Crushed in silent daze,
The suffering of a lonely world
Wrapped in the latest craze
Of war.

EF, 1994.

Love

Love blossoms through every window
Through every pane of glass,
Love blossoms through every season
Through every blade of grass.
Love blossoms on every mountain
Through every moor,
Love blossoms for those who are rich
And for those who are poor.

EF, 1994.

Advice

Listen, young people doing exams
Don't be led away like lambs,
To follow those who deal in drugs
Who ruin lives and live like thugs,
But do your work, make a decision
To sit down early and do revision
Remember, seeds you sow today
Should never lead your lives astray.

EF, 1994.

Troubles

It's hard to believe that the troubles are gone
No more bullets, no more bombs.
It's hard to believe after twenty-five years
That we've no more crying, no more tears.
Who could have thought in all that time
There'd be so much suffering, so much crime?

EF, 1995.

Mackies

At sixteen years I started work in Belfast,
Mackies' foundry.
Like a lamb out to the slaughter, unfamiliar
With the boundary.
I got a bus at 7.10, that took me to the station
And walked the rest, the Springfield Road, my heart in palpitation.
For we started work at ten to eight, the hooter it would sound,
"And dare you not be late my boy, or you'll be homeward bound".
The factory it was full of men, they were scattered all around,
Most of them they walked it home 'cause
They came from Belfast town.
But I, a little country lad, Apprentice to my trade,
Rode my bike, got a bus and walked
To make the grade.
I swore I'd be an engineer and make a million pounds,
And have the biggest, finest house
Led out on fancy grounds.
That's how it was when I was young, all those years ago
You dreamt of things you never had and longed to see them grow,
You heard your parents and others say,
That work was number one,
"So you just strive to do your best, young Fullerton".

EF, 1995.

Time

When he married her she was
His wife, and lover, all in one.
Together they were happy
And in time they had a son.
Then a daughter came along
A lovely little girl,
She filled their lives with great content
As every day unfurled.
Another girl would make it three.
And soon the years rolled by,
It wasn't very long till
They were standing eye to eye.
When he married her
His hair was brown
And she thought her curls would stay,
But now they stand on common ground
For both their heads are grey.

EF, 1996.

The Accordion Player

I saw her way up in the distance, on a windowsill she sat,
She was playing an old accordion
And on the footpath was her hat.
She had a ring in her ear, and one in her nose,
And her hair tied back in a plait,
She looked so very contented
On the windowsill she sat.

I pondered a while on the footpath,
As she gracefully moved her two arms,
And the beautiful tune she was playing
Was so sweet: 'Those Endearing Young Charms',
I can hardly describe the young talent
As her music it filled up my ears,
For one minute my cheeks they were smiling
And then in my eyes there were tears.

On my own sure I thought I was staring,
As I fleeced through my coat for a coin,
I lifted my eyes up to heaven,
There were hundreds all standing around,
Some were clapping, some stood there in silence,
There were people of every class,
I was glad of my visit to Dublin, just to witness this musical lass.

EF, 1997.

The Flu

Each day is just a struggle,
From you wake up at the dawn,
Trying to motivate your body,
And tell your mind to "Get a move on".

Your arms and legs are aching,
From your toils the day before,
You would think your bones were shrinking
For you've pains high up and lower.

Your head is even sore to touch,
There's cramps in every joint,
You try to bend to tie your lace
And grunt, "Sure what the hell's the point?"

But soon the penny drops
You put your hands up to your head,
"There'll be no work for me today",
As you crawl back into bed.

EF, 1997.

The Hospital

They've closed the doors of the hospital,
They've switched out all the lights,
The over-paid at the top of the scale
Have deprived us all of our rights,
They've turned off all the heating,
And they've emptied all the beds,
And they're telling us to travel
To other places instead.

And now the walls that echoed out
A voice to those unwell,
Stands looking out across the town
No more than an empty shell.
The people all who worked there
Have spread their wings and flew,
For the sound of closure filled their ears
They knew the doom was true.

EF, 1997.

Mum and Dad's 'Golden'

They got married 4th February 1948,
Soon Eileen came along, November was the date,
Both of them had hard to work,
They had to toe the line.
Then our Christina came along in 1949.

The time it passed so quickly
And it wasn't always fun,
But Rita she was born in 1951.
As you will now have noticed
Three girls have come their way
And for a little boy mum said my Da would pray
When sure as God out of the blue
Eugene he was born in 1952.

Now things did not get easier
The house was like a beehive,
When Miriam came along, in 1955.
Well if you think I'm finished,
Then let me put the record straight,
For our wee sister Bernie was born 1958.

Oh now it's not all over,
Let me take you back in time,
For our dear brother Seamus appeared in 1959.
Well,now that I've reached seven
You'll be say'n that's all the fun,
Well no its not, Patricia was born in 1961.

Now you can all imagine the houseful that we had,
And although it wasn't easy they were cheery mum and dad,
But anyway the fun it stopped in 1968
When mum and dad they parted 20 years from that first date.

The next ten years were very hard; he talked about her fate,
How he walked to Pleasant Bank, and met her at the gate.
So hard it was for him indeed, he was always in a state,
To finally in March that year he died in '78.
So I'd like us to remember them, as all of us we grow,
When '98 approaches… It was 50 years ago. (*EF, 1998*).

Business Mind

I started my own business in September '79,
Determined the decisions of the future would be mine,
And I shook hands with my boss and said that "I'm away!"
He told me he was sorry and tried to make me stay.

But I had made my mind up the time for me was right,
And nothing he could offer me would make me change my sight,
For a vision in my mind was the path I had to go
I decided I would make it, hail, rain, snow or blow.

So I built myself a shed and I battered and I bled,
And I vowed that I would make it on my own.
Every hour of day I'd toil, I would burn the midnight oil,
Price the work, do the job, and use the phone.

Now the time it flew for me, I was busy as a bee,
I was happy working morning, noon and night,
Every man came through the gate; it was never, ever late,
A customer for sure was in my sight.

And so I plodded on till number six was born,
And the years were disappearing from my life,
'Till one day I realised standing there before my eyes
The children all the same size as my wife.

So I've slowed it down a hush and decided not to rush,
And to take the time to give my folks a smile,
Now I try to work to live, just enough for me to give,
My time to them, for just a short, short while.

EF, 2000.

The Engagement

A young couple from Belfast went courting,
To the sea side at Bangor each week,
And after a month or two talking,
He gave her a peck on the cheek.

They would drive down the road every evening,
And park his wee car by the sea,
And after a year or two courting,
He placed his hand firm on her knee.

Then a ring he soon placed on her finger,
She was flattered as she could be,
She said, "Darling engagement is bonding",
You can put *both* your hands on my knee!"

So last week as they sat there together,
In Bangor down by the blue sea,
She said, "You may go somewhat further",
So he drove on to Donaghadee.

EF, 2000.

That's not a Lion!

A young man walked into a bar-room,
A Giraffe on a lead in his hand,
He walked right across to the barmaid
And here they proceeded to stand.

Now he ordered a pint and a halfin',
One for him and one for his friend,
And after an hour or twos drinking,
The giraffe's neck it started to bend.

Very soon they were pissed from the boozing,
And the giraffe it slumped down on the floor,
The young man trying to flee from it snoozing,
Headed out and made straight for the door.

With a mouthful of beer, "Don't leave that ly'n here",
Cried someone with a very loud laugh,
But your man at the door yelled back with a roar,
"That's not a lion, that's a giraffe!"

EF, 2000.

The Fiddle

My daddy played the fiddle at the fire side every night,
He'd rosin up the bow and make sure all the strings were tight.
He'd then invite my sisters out to dance upon the floor,
The reels were fast, the jigs were class, the horn pipes, they were slower.

My daddy played the fiddle in the very early morn,
I would follow him with buckets to fill the bag with corn,
He'd then head off across the soil his arm going to and fro
To carefully sow the seeds the earth would finally grow.

My daddy played two fiddles, each one had a unique sound,
When he played the first one the neighbours gathered round,
He'd fill our house with music and all would clap and fling,
The bow upon the strings would make the fiddle sing.

Now when he played the second one, you just could never tell,
For daddy in his hey day could play them both so well,
And even in the early morn when no one stood around,
The music played to cast the seed into its earthly ground.

EF, 1992-2002.

Work Blues

When you stop to think of the speed of time,
It just disappears like an old clocks chime,
It fades away like a summer tan,
Old folks say 'Time waits on no man'.

When you push the world in front of you,
And labour and toil 'til your face is blue,
It's true again what old folks say,
You're just wishing and wasting your time away.

So stop and think every now and then,
Take a step back every now and again,
And remember once more what old folks say,
Try to live a little along the way.

Before you know it'll be over and done,
So take the time for a little fun,
And ponder back to days gone by,
When old folks even had the time to die.

EF, 2003.

Moon

Oh what a moon,
What a glorious moon,
Suspended from the sky,
You urge me just to look at you,
From your cradle way up high,

When you are round,
And bright and full,
There's nothing can surpass,
The beauty in your smiling face,
Would shame any darling lass.

EF, 2004.

Three Cheers for Lent

This man he sat in a neat wee pub,
And he ordered his usual three beers,
He would then sit down at a table
And proceed to drink it with "Cheers".

Now this man he was known as a reg'lar,
Every night without fail he'd appear,
And without any fuss or much to discuss,
He would empty his three pints of beer.

Now one night an observant young barmaid,
Very nimbly approached this dear man,
She asked him to answer her question,
And he said, "Sure, I will if I can".

She said, "You come here every night of the year,
And three pints you put out of sight,
I'd just like to know why you come here and buy,
And then just get up and take flight?"

"Well", he said, "My dear miss, the truth is like this,
Sure it's simple if you listen a while,
I've a brother in Boston and one in New York
And I toast their good health with a smile".

So one night this young maid, she was nearly afraid,
To ask why, he should buy only two.
But in her usual way, she proceeded to say,
"Has one brother? Has he passed away?"

"Ach, no, my dear lass", as he lifted his glass,
"Sure it's the time of the year that God sent,
My promise is true and I'll drink only two
For I'm off the oul drink for Lent!"

EF, 2004.

Nappy Times

You would never see a nappy now, hanging on the line,
It used to be you'd come across them, nearly all the time.
Three or four and even more, we'd wash them every day,
Put them on the babies' bums, some Ariel white, some grey.

Nearly every parent had them, a dozen and even more,
They were used to wipe the table, used to dry the floor,
They'd be hanging round the fireplace,
when the rain was in the air,
You could see them on the mantle piece and draped behind a chair.

And when they turned from white to grey,
with washing every day,
You could use them then as dusters,
to keep spiders' webs at bay.
And in the end when all would fray, too rough for babies' skin,
You'd gather up the worst ones and chuck them in the bin.

But you'd never see a nappy now, hanging on the line,
Three or four to wash, sure they wouldn't take the time.
People now spend twice as long tramping round the shops,
Looking for the throwaways to use as babies' mops!

EF, 2005.

Jamie's

We followed on from Tinnelly's men,
Who stripped the roof today,
Asbestos now is dangerous, or so the experts say,
It's been there like, for 30 years,
And it hasn't caused no harm,
It was used in shops and factories,
And even on the farm,

But we had to get the new roof on, and all within the day,
So with crane on site and weather bright,
We had an overcoat to lay.
We hoisted up the sheets, a bundle at a time,
And sweated from the inside out,
To spread them in a line.

Overhead it's nice and dry, but drizzle is forecast,
And I'll be really hoping, that the worst of it has passed,
For fitting up a roof is hard enough to do,
Without a slippery surface,
That could leave you in the stew.

But with every sheet that covers, leaves a meter less to do,
And the harder that you graft means you soon have very few,
So you tape them and screw them, and fit the laps down tight,
And before you even know it, you'll be running out of light,
For the days are very short now, at this time of the year,
You have to keep your head down and stay there in first gear.

As you're coming to the last sheet and the dark is falling down,
You put the tek into the gun and screw it through the crown,
That only leaves the flashings and the ridge to seal it in,
We gather up the cuttings and scrap them in the bin.
And then you take a deep breath and thank the Lord up high,
Another roof completed, looking up towards the sky.

EF, January 31ˢᵗ 2005.

If I Could Find a Way to Say I'm Sorry (Song)

If I could find a way to say I'm sorry,
For all the hurtful things that I have said,
If I could only turn the clock back darling,
I would tell you that I love you more instead.

It started with a silly row this morning,
I said some things that I know were untrue,
I never dreamt I could be so uncaring,
It scares me just to think what I can do.

You asked me such a simple little question,
And of course I nearly snapped the head off you.
It was almost like the devil in me testing,
How far that I could push you through and through?

If I could find a way to say I'm sorry,
For all the hurtful things that I have said,
If I could only turn the clock back darling,
I would tell you that I love you more instead.

It was later on that day when I next saw you,
You greeted me with such amazing grace,
You said the past was over and forgave me,
I will always see your lovely smiling face.

If I could find a way to say I'm sorry,
For all the hurtful things that I have said,
If I could only turn the clock back darling,
I would tell you that I love you more instead.

EF, 2005.

Praying Time

Sometimes I get sick of praying,
As if it's a waste of time,
So I just stop and say, "No more",
It's there I draw the line.

Then I take the time and plan my day,
And tell God what I'll do,
I try to smile and have a laugh,
And I hear God laughing too.

The dawn leads on too quick to noon,
And soon it passes three,
It's not too long before I know,
That He's laughing straight at me,

For God has seen it all before,
He lets me have my way,
He knows that I'll be back to Him,
Before the end of day.

EF, 2005.

Morning Love Blues

When I wake up every morning, drag myself up from my bed,
Sometimes I can't remember what I've done and said,
So I call you on the phone, and I tell you I am sorry,
For going away and leaving you, leaving you all alone.
Then I know that you still love me,
When you say, that you'll come home.

    (Chorus)
Coming home to me dear, coming home to me,
Coming home to me here, coming to see me,
Loving me again, loving me forever.
Trying to forget the past, hoping it won't last,
Loving me tomorrow, loving me today,
Trying to remember you in every way.

For I never should have left you, and you should never have left me,
But the love we had together was just never meant to be.
For when love decides to pass you, there isn't any shame,
So remember when the tide turns, that no one was to blame,
So I walk away in sorrow, just to try and ease the pain,
And I know that come tomorrow, I might not see you again.

    (Chorus)
Coming home to me dear, coming home to me,
Coming home to me here, coming to see me,
Loving me again, loving me forever
Trying to forget the past, hoping it won't last,
Loving me tomorrow loving me today,
Trying to remember you in every way.

EF, 2005.

Steel Sizes

Steel beams and RSJs
I see them in my sleep,
Columns, angles, flat bars too,
Out from the ceiling leap.

Measurements and details rush
All through my head at night,
Cold formed hollow sections
Sometimes stiffen me with fright.

I see structural steel and hot rolled plate
And zinc coated sheets in piles,
I see railings, gates and purlins,
Stretched out by the mile.

There's aluminium durbar plate
Wire mesh, all shapes and sizes,
You never seem to have enough,
No matter how much you buy-es.

EF, 2005.

Epitaph

Once I lived and now I don't,
Done my own thing, now I won't.
Have to stay here in my grave,
No matter what I cannot leave.
Got no TV, got no phone,
I just lie here all alone.
Twenty four long hours a day,
Ne'er a word I cannot say.
So think of me and don't ask who,
'Cause someday you will lie here too.

EF, 2008.

The 23 Parishes of Diocese of Dromore

Aghaderg and Annaclone
    lying side by side,
Burren and Clonduff
    from each other trying to hide,
Dromore and Dromara,
Drumgath and Donaghmore,
Then there's the two Drumgooland's
    higher up and lower,
Kilbroney's at the bottom
    just beside the bay,
With Mayobridge and Magheradroll
    from each other miles away.
Moyraverty and Magheralin,
    they're not so far apart,
But to get yourself to Newry
    you must make an early start,
There's Seapatrick and there's Seagoe,
St Peter and St Paul's,
Then you head on up to Saval
    where they built a nice new hall,
Then back up north to Tullylish
    in alphabetical order,
You finally head to Warrenpoint
    up near beside the border.

EF, 2005.

Question time

How do you stop time from passing? they say,
Do you take all the clocks and throw them away?
How do you freeze the years that decay?
Do you put them on ice and hope that they stay?
What do you do when your hair starts to stray,
Or changes its colours from ginger to grey?
How do you change the way people age,?
Do you turn the book back, page after page?
How do we alter the way that we look,
Or take back the youth the years have just took?
How do you turn off the pains that you feel?
As your body gets older from head down to heel?
How do you mind all the things your ma said,
Do you stop watching tv and read more instead?
How do you stop all the things in your head,
From turning to dust before you are dead?

Well from writing this poem I've come to believe,
That dwelling on life could turn you to grieve,
So take a deep breath and don't feel so dull,
It's the candle that's withered that has lived to the full.

EF, 2008

Prayer

Lord, cleanse my heart and cleanse my soul
And cleanse my tongue and all,
Keep the sins of day at bay
So I won't sin at all.

Do not allow the stains that stick
To every part of me,
But use your elbow grace, oh Lord,
So all from me, will flee.

Wash out my mouth with your rough sea
To choose the words that flow from me,
Do not allow my heart to stray
And keep the evil thoughts at bay.

Above all else, it's fair to say
That I will do my best today,
So on my tongue and in my soul
Along with You I'll always stroll.

EF, 2005.

A Name

There's a name on every face,
And a face to every name,
It's how you recognize that
Everybody's not the same.
It determines who you are,
From the day that you are born,
And it stays with you forever,
Even though your body's worn.
If you try to live without it,
There's no future and no fame,
No one would even speak to you,
Cause they wouldn't know your name.

EF, 2006.

Happy Days 1962

Stories by the number,
Annals by the score,
There are so many memories
I could tell you more and more,
For we were showered with freedom,
Endless days of hours to spare,
The troubles of the passing world
We never shared a care.

We got going to the threshers
Though our mothers weren't so keen,
They could always see the dangers
That our fathers never seen,
We could sit behind a tractor
High up on the bales of hay,
And we never felt the boredom
Young ones say they feel today.

Well the sun was always shining
Way back then the sky was blue,
We were always plotting something
There were endless things to do,
But there's been some revolutions
Since the days that we were young,
It's hard to take it in today
How much the world has swung.

EF, January 2009.

Reincarnation

Now I don't believe in reincarnation
It's not something I've thought much about,
I have never seriously ever discussed it
So I've never been in any doubt.

But I heard this wee story of Andy,
He always would drink in the pub,
And in between drinking his whiskeys
Oul songs they would flow from his gub.

Now one day a small group of drinkers
Were debating the spiritual world,
The possibility of reincarnation
It surely began to unfold.

Now the barman was asked his opinion,
They were anxious his knowledge to know,
He glanced his eyes over to Andy
And said, "He will come back as a crow."

Now Andy was fond of his singing
But he also was fond of the beer,
He took a quick look at the barman
And he said to him, "You listen here…"

"If a crow is what I come back as
Then happy I will be with my lot,
For I will park myself up on your chimney
And songs I will sing down your pot".

EF, January 2009.

Climate Changes

Rathfriland on the hill
January early and the day is very still,
The sun it was reflecting across the water tower,
The shadows on the concrete
Displayed its awesome powers,
In the square where we were busy, people stood in New Year talk,
While the eagle eyed for bargains
Around the shops they walked.

But what I want to emphasize to all who read these lines,
Is there really such a difference
With all our changing times?
For today the sun is shining as it was those years ago,
With the talk of global warming
And the steep decline in snow,
Well I am not an expert when it comes to climate change,
But looking back those twenty years
It seems that much remains.

For today the sun is shining as it was in eighty nine,
In fact the glare is so intense
We had to draw the blinds,
And yet for all that I recall I strongly must admit,
There surely must be something
Even though great minds are split,
For every year when we were young
The sleighs were oiled and greased,
You were sure of frost and snow for months
Before the winter eased.

So I'm back to where I started, for I don't know what to think,
And yet it must be proven for there has to be a link,
And even take this winter past we had little frost or snow,
And today the sun is shining
Well the experts, they must know.

EF, January 2009.

The Steel Lorry

The Lorry, all twenty five tonnes of it
The trailer twisted its wheels in our yard,
The tyres squealed and flattened
On the concrete, rock hard.

The springs yelled as in deep distress
With the shear weight load under duress,
The brakes released from the pressure
Like this massive air refresher.

The chains tensioned to the limits
No shortcuts, no brief ways to trim it,
Restrained any movements in the beams
Taken seriously, even to the extremes.

The lorry, all twenty five tonnes of it
Prepared well for anything unforeseen,
Leaves our yard, pivots on the load
To take on the busy occupied roads.

EF, January 2009.

Wild desires

The roads that we all drive on
Remind me of a monster,
They take every opportunity
To gobble up our youngsters,
You can almost hear it laughing
Through lungs of flaming fire,
There is plenty in abundance
To fulfil my wild desires.

They're dressed in black just waiting
Made up of stones and tar,
No concern for make or model
They'll devour most any car,
They tempt you with their straightness
Provoke you with their bends,
They love to hear you speeding
And they thrive on long weekends.

They are always being resurfaced
Just to make them smooth and flat,
To lie in wait and lick their lips
And smile like a Cheshire cat,
But the roads are deadly places
And a life is the monsters meal,
So for God's sake pay attention
Keep your both hands on the wheel.

EF, February 2009.

The Black Hearse

I overtook it on the motorway
One way, there's no returning,
It had all the signs
Without the writing
Which spelled the last journey.

No prizes for guessing the colour,
No rewards for who was inside,
A reminder of that final journey
And for now the remains to reside.

A vehicle that looked so familiar
Enough room in the back just for one,
The starkest reminders to viewers
Of a life that is over and done.

On the motorway this medium was moving
The last journey was going my way
The inevitable truth in the coffin,
To be grateful I'm living today.

No return from the voyage he's making
Sure the ticket it's only one way,
No fragrance or scent from the flowers
On his own, in his coffin, he lay.

EF, February 2009.

The Fox

Straggled and bedraggled
All his ribs were clear to see,
Not giving in to hunger in pursuit, in agony,
He follows her relentlessly
There is no turning back,
No amount of pain or anguish
Will throw him off his track.

The length of day not matters
The dark of night more still,
The beginning of a journey,
He knows he must fulfil,
With nature as his driving force
And instinct his desire,
The need to breed and spread his seed
Is all that he requires.

But not until she's ready
And that could be another week,
She's prepared to keep him waiting
Despite his weak physique,
But he can't take the risk of not
Being there, just him alone,
All of his adversaries, his job is to dethrone.

So trapped inside this waiting game
He's there to the bitter end,
Just waiting for the second
To become her mating friend,
For the length of day not matters
And the dark of night more still,
The ending of a journey
He was determined to fulfil.

EF, February 2009.

If Truth Be Told

What a world this here could be
If lies from peoples mouths would flee,
And what a difference this could make
If truth be told for honest sake.

"I'm sure the cheque is in the post,
For I licked the stamp myself",
When knowing bluntly all the time
It's sitting on the shelf.

What a change to people's lives
When everything that's good arrives,
To hold your hands above your head
And bet your life on all you said.

"I'll phone you back, give you my word",
No sooner said than done,
When all the time you know damn well
Another white lie spun.

What a world this here could be
If tongue in cheek could only see,
The damage caused by all the lies,
That honest people multiply.

EF, March 2009.

Blue Tit Beauty

There's a lovely little blue tit
Eating nuts outside our front,
And it's totally oblivious
To a prowler on the hunt,
For it twists and turns
And spends it's time
Hanging upside down,
It is totally unaware
Of a cat that hangs around.

Now this lovely little blue tit
Has invited all its friends,
Like wasps around a jam pot
On the nut bag they ascend,
And like scavengers on a carcass
The contents disappear
In the front, and twice as quick
It all comes out the rear.

But some are over anxious
In their zest to fill up full,
And they fail to pay attention
They are so digestible,
They over look the hidden eyes
That makes them such good prey,
With lighting speed, a greedy cat
Can easily end their days.

EF, March 2009.

Suck, Don't Blow

I have got this little harmonica,
A 'mouth organ' some people would say,
It's nice to be able to pick it up
And sit down for a tune to play.

Now it works between sucking and blowing
And it produces a very good sound,
It fits neatly right into your pocket
And it's easy to carry around.

Now I learned to play from my father
Who sat me in front of his face,
You know they say 'Practice makes Perfect',
For soon I could play any place.

Sometimes we would play them together
Remembering to suck and to blow,
He always thought mine sounded better
'Til one day he said, "Give me a go".

"What way are you playing this fiddle?"
For that's what he called it sometimes,
"Good God", he exclaimed to his horror
"You're holding it the opposite way round".

Yes, the notes that he played to his left side
Were the same notes as mine to the right
The price paid for facing each other
Well, we're not going to change it tonight.

EF, March 2009.

Empty Pockets, Rich Promises.

Whether there's two at your funeral
Or two thousand is irrelevant,
Little matters who will come to this event,
Be them rich or be them poor
It makes no difference, that's for sure,
Your life will not be judged
By who has went.

Now when someone is well known
And renowned for all their wealth,
They may be highly spoken of by us,
People take a half a day
Just to gather round and pray,
And in some ways they create
A lot of fuss.

But when some poor ladies soul
Lies forgotten in a home,
Passes on, there's not so many making noise,
It makes no difference if you're seen
Or at the funeral you have been,
For this person never had
No blue eyed boys.

So if you should die unknown
Or if you should die in wealth
On this journey you will travel on your own,
For this final destination
Does not depend on admiration,
In front of God
We all will stand alone.

EF, March 2009.

My Neighbour

Tuesday was my last visit,
My last time to ever see her,
I peeped through the window,
She was dosing in the chair.

I don't know if she sensed me
But she seemed to waken up,
I tapped softly on the pane
Not to startle her or the empty cup.

Slowly and with frailty she arrived
Opening the latch she welcomed me,
Her smile always apart from the pain
She kept hidden, but obvious to see.

"Not great" was her response
To my, "How are you today?"
"Not great, but sure I'll not complain":
Words she often used to pray.

Little did I know sitting facing her
That it would be my last time,
Although the weakness was there
She still made the effort to shine.

So I left her after about an hour,
Hoping, but knowing her strength was gone,
It was only days before I missed her
The company I'd known for so long.

EF, 31ˢᵗ March 2009.

The Boundaries of Love

Love it knows no boundaries
When it comes to family flesh,
You would try to move a mountain
Just to give them good advice.

Kindness and devotion,
Fondness, warmth and care,
Qualities overtaking
You're just waiting there to share.

Experience in abundance,
You try to give away,
Knowing it will stand by them
Their lives will never stray.

Friendship and affection
You will shower upon their heads,
Mistakes you'll overlook
And give them confidence instead.

And when it comes to sharing love,
No one is left unturned,
And hopefully too many times
Their spirits will not be burned.

EF, April 2009.

Temptation

Oh gentle hand console me
As you touch against my skin,
Oh gentle God forgive me
In the midst of thoughts of sin,
Oh fingers flesh caress so fresh
And feel my heart beat strong,
Oh feelings, quick persuade me
That I can do no wrong.

Oh gentle mind release me
From thoughts perverse today,
Oh eyes of observation
Hesitate not, turn away,
Oh serious inclinations heed
And don't be lured in dreams,
Oh strange desires and passion fires
Lead me through trips extreme.

Oh gentle soul direct me
From libido, lust and crave,
Oh gentle spirit accompany me
And raise me from the grave,
Oh grace that once surrounded me
Persuade me to aspire,
Oh gentle flame that burns within
Please conquer my desires.

EF, April 2009.

Negative Equity

Negative equity, what does it mean
To the ordinary man on the street?
We all know him
Maybe you are him,
Always trying to make ends meet.

It seems to be the two top words
That's used on the news right now,
While thousands suffer vision blurred
They're stuck with sweating brow.

For simply what it means is this
What you bought is far too dear,
If you went to sell then the emphasis
Dictates that loud and clear.

You bought a house two hundred grand
Too expensive from the start,
Now, your head is in the sand,
With bleeding in your heart.

There's nothing you can do this day
Just try to hold on tight,
Don't try to sell or give away
Everything will be alright,
The hardships we must all endure
For we are all the same,
When all of us feel insecure
We've only ourselves to blame.

EF, April 2009.

Titanic's Early Grave

She was designated 401, the longest ever built,
At forty six thousand, she was tonnage to the hilt,
And when she slid down gantries into icy Belfast Lough
She had only one ambition, her voyage to New York.

It was on the 31st of May the year nineteen eleven
One hundred thousand people watched
And witnessed sights from heaven,
They yelled and cheered and flew their flags
As each one held their breath,
No one could have predicted
She was within one year of death.

Her bulkheads they were iron strong
Her hull was double skinned,
With space enough between the layers
A man could stand up in,
And although the word 'unsinkable'
Was never actually used,
Most people did believe it now, let no one be confused.

Well despite the little hiccup when she struck HMS Hawke,
Titanic passed the sea trials
She would soon be bound for Cork,
And when her time it finally came
To Southampton Port of call,
This enormous White Star liner,
She roared out from chimneys tall.

She headed on to Queenstown; it is now the cove of Cork,
With many fine rich people she would soon be in New York,
Two thousand, two hundred passengers
And crew were on that ship,
The fifth day of her voyage
The world would soon be gripped.

It was April 14th nineteen twelve,
Her knots were twenty two,
She was skimming through the water
Like a dolphin nearly new,
The hour was almost midnight
When a monster cold as ice,
It just appeared from nowhere
Its position was precise.

It scraped her hull like a raging bull,
Three hundred feet and more,
The rivets popped, the steel plates flopped,
She was sailing at deaths door,
They called for Thomas Andrews, he was the Engineer,
Examining the damage, he was surely struck with fear,
"We only have two hours", he said,
"This tragic ship is doomed",
Already she is crying out in agonising tunes.

Two twenty was the fatal hour
Titanic's stern gapped to the sky,
With fifteen hundred people still on board
They all would die,
With flickering lights and crashing sounds
She slipped beneath the waves
Seven hundred souls survived that night
As she slid to her early grave.

EF, April 2009.

Titanic's Fate

On the fourteenth of April Nineteen and twelve,
The titanic disappeared,
Unable to withstand the blow, the impact so severe,
It was on her maiden voyage that the structural Engineer,
Thomas Andrews, told the Captain
For his ship the end was near.
She'd struck a solid block of ice of twenty times her size,
It tore the rivets from her hull, her inside was baptized,
The passengers they were sleeping, unaware below the decks,
That the engines were abandoned
By the men, to save their necks.

For the forces of the water, a thousand tonnes or more,
Had ripped her side wide open, and burst her strongest doors,
Despite her being unsinkable, her fate was signed and sealed,
Atlantic it would swallow her, this great Titanic meal.
A hundred years has passed almost since she was so conceived,
In Belfast yard three thousand men, infallible they believed,
For nothing had been built so large to brave the ocean waves,
Titanic was the greatest, she would live beyond the grave.

It's not what they expected though that she should die so soon,
And certainly in her prime of life, not on her honeymoon,
But time has proven different, the 'berg she could not match,
The ocean waves were opened, this massive beast to catch.
There were only twenty life boats onboard this huge big ship
To deal with such a tragedy she was simply ill-equipped,
But no one in this world could have predicted to this day
Titanic's life would end so soon not in this tragic way.
And so it was, it came to pass, Titanic lived no more,
She lay beneath the ocean waves like many ships before,
But praise to those who built her, she was superior in every way,
If she hadn't hit that iceberg, she could still be here today.

EF, April 2009.

Titanic Memories

There are many great occurrences embedded in our minds,
It's strange how we remember them
The dates we can unwind,
The shooting of JF Kennedy, 'most everyone can recall,
The date of the battle of Hastings
You cannot forget at all.

We remember the day Diana died and Mother Teresa too,
The men who landed on the moon,
Well, him and you know who,
And there's many more occasions that each one has in store,
Enshrined in our great memories
For now and evermore.

But it always seems to be the case that one surrounds our time,
The voyage of Titanic
Just sends chills right down our spines,
For it totally has encaptured our obsessions with the past,
Transfixed by its proportion
And its demanding will to last.

For Titanic was a mammoth craft she was built in Belfast town,
She enlisted all the services
From thousands all around,
They clocked in every morning, their talents to combine,
To build this massive iron giant
Of structure and design.

Well Titanic sailed and Titanic sunk before my dad was born,
And yet we're all ensnared by her,
For those who drowned we mourn,
For when she hit the iceberg and sank beneath the waves,
She enshrined herself in history
Generations to enslave. E.F. April 2009

Cool, Cool Water

Hold your hands under a drinking tap
Let the cold water freshen your palms,
Splash it all over your cheek bones
And enjoy its life-giving charms.

Clamp your hands tightly with pressure,
Cup them up firm like a bowl,
Allow the soft texture of nature
Flow perfectly into your soul.

Shake your hands dry from the moisture
Allow them to drain on your skin,
Renewed with the spirit of the liquid
Absorbed on the tissues within.

Rub your hands gently together
And appreciate what you have done,
Let your mind flow in cool water,
The greatest thing under the sun.

Observe your hands, clean and refreshing,
A miracle has flowed from the earth,
It's something we can't take for granted
So rejoice in its everyday birth.

EF, April 2009.

Once Only a Man

"Once a man and twice a child"
I heard this from my dad,
I used to wonder what he meant
When I was just a lad.

But as the years crept on me
And I left my youth behind,
I understood the words much more
The meaning I could find.

For once he was a strong made man
His body stood the test,
He dedicated all his skills
He could keep up with the rest.

But as the years sped onwards
He grew frail as people do,
No more his hands upon the plough
Those days were through and through.

And when at last he lay there
Much too weak to even smile,
I remember what he said to me
"Once a man and twice a child"

EF, April 2009.

Mirror Reflection

Stop for a minute and look in the mirror
And reflect on the face you're staring at there,
How it has changed in all of the years
With many a headache, worries and fears.

For once when you stared what did you see?
A youthful reflection, the image of me,
With no indications that life was to pass
A portrait of beauty there on the glass.

Without hesitation you'd drain away time
Absorbing for hours yourself in your prime,
From different hair-dos to cleaning your teeth
With over indulgence, that beggars belief.

But now when you're gapping its wrinkles you see
A big spot in a crevice is staring at thee,
And bags that refuse to hide under your eyes
Looking at skin, that resembles deep fries.

There's hairs in your nose now, hairs in your ears
Trim them and clip them, they just reappear,
And then the wee thread veins they ever increase
Letting you know what the years can release.

But all is not lost now, for more can be found
Your eyes can still see, your ears hear the sound,
The tongue is still speaking, the smell in your nose
Be thankful to God that your age it still shows.

EF, April 2009.

85

The Disappeared

They took away my lovely son
And stole him from my heart,
They put a hood around his head
And tore my life apart.

My son he never had a chance
To say goodbye to me,
They laid him in a shallow grave
Beside some weeping tree.

And in the head they shot my son
The bullet pierced the clay,
With conscience free, no thought for me
They buried him that day.

And there alone they left my son
Where no one else could find,
How often we have looked for him
With eyes so dim and blind.

The years have past with you my son
Although we can not see,
Beside you there each day I'll stay
The pain will always be.

But I still live in hope, my son
For the silent days to end,
Our family plot to lay you in
Where we can all attend.

EF, May2009.

Gordon

Sometimes words are meaningless
Because they don't mean what they say,
Unless when someone speaking them
Does so in a truthful way.

And when I cast my mind back
Back in time some twenty years,
I just find it very difficult
To control the flow of tears

For never in my life before
Did I hear such language spoke,
Those words from Gordon Wilson
This father's heart was broke.

His words were for his daughter
Whose lifeless corpse lay still,
When quizzed about her killers said,
"I bare them no ill will".

Expressions of this nature
Had not been heard before,
To grant someone forgiveness
"Was to even up the score"

The words they spread like wildfire
Old ways were to depart,
A totally new beginning
Arose in peoples' hearts.

EF, May 2009.

Balls of Brass

"It would freeze the balls off a brass monkey",
I would hear my mother say,
She would tell us brave and often
On a cold and winters day,
But we were far too young then
To understand her ways,
It was better not to question,
Best explained another day.

So the monkey's balls were frozen
In our minds for many years,
The words were never spoke of
And disappeared with mother dear,
But recently the cobwebs cleared
At a family get-together,
When talking of those times of old,
We remembered that bad weather.

Well, the riddle has been solved now:
They were fixed on sailing ships,
They were used to stack the cannon balls
So the guns were well equipped,
And when the ship sailed out to sea
In the rain and frost and snow,
The temperature would always drop
To minus and below,

The cannon balls they shrunk in size
On the monkeys made of brass,
Fell off and rolled across the decks:
So the saying came to pass.

Believe it or believe it not!

EF, May 2009.

Funeral Eulogy

I am gone now, I am dead
This life for me is done,
There is only so much time for us,
For each and every one.

I don't have all the answers
And indeed I would not try,
Just except that this is God's will
That life has passed me by.

On earth I tried to do my best
Beside you all I stood,
If I could stay another while
You know in truth I would.

But that is not the way things are
Some events we cannot change,
We must accept the deal we got,
Despite however strange.

Not one of us escapes the net:
The big fish and the small,
The good, the bad, the in-between,
Life catches up with all.

So let things sit the way they are
For the time will soon go by,
And in the end for all of us
Our time will come to die.

EF, May 2009.

Bygone Chores 1960

I carried water from the well
To wash the spuds I gathered,
Poured some into the blackberries
To weigh them up, we bothered,
Spent the evenings after school
Tying hay and sheaving,
Papa fixing peoples' boots
With needle thread a-weaving.

Helping mother wash the clothes
Steeped in a big steel basin,
Rasping them against the sides
The stains of youth embracing,
Then twisting and removing them
To rinse them in the river,
Before the final cleansing
Our little hands would shiver.

Scores of chores we licked our sores
And we headed off to bed,
Usually on our hands and knees
So cold the sheets were spread,
But clambered up together
We could soon turn up the heat,
Underneath the blankets
We would warm each others feet.

EF, May 2009.

The Damning

The day is breaking, steeped in sins
The damning of our church begins,
Industrial schools have hit the map
While hearts and souls and tempers snap.

The years of tears ensnared with fears
Have finally opened up deaf ears,
To bring alive the evil crimes
And serve them up to present times.

To focus on, without excuse,
The terrible plague of child abuse,
With everyday a story new
To turn your stomach up in spew.

We blame the church, we blame the state,
We look for souls to implicate,
We search for ways to vengeance seek
Which leaves us all with an evil streak.

But we must turn to God instead
That this has raised its ugly head,
And pray in thanks and hope and praise
To see us through this horrible phase.

For we can't change what has been done
What would we gain if all was won?
So let us strive to share the pain
And don't hold on to history's stains.

EF, 20th May 2009.

Driving Mad

If you're thinking of changing your motorcar
And you're considering what you should get,
Then maybe you should have a good look
But don't buy anything yet.

For driving is worse than it used to be
There's a lot more things to confront,
Especially those obstacle pot-holes
That leave your teeth bearing the brunt.

And then there's the muck to contend with
That's trailed out of every ploughed field,
They just never consider commuters
When driving their massive four wheels.

So before you should contemplate models
You are wishing to place on the road,
Remember the muck and the pot-holes
On the highway that break every code.

For it might be a worthwhile suggestion
In fact it could be the right thought,
To cope with the every frustration
A Ferguson tractor is bought.

So if you think of replacing your motor
Think long before you should change,
To cope with the holes and the muck,
'John Deere' keep the top of the range.

EF, May 2009.

Free For All

No day can be as wonderful
As the day that brings the sun,
It brightens all and everything
As it shines on everyone.

You wake up in the morning
And the grass is crisp and dry,
The gutters they are cracking
As if to wave the rain goodbye.

And everybody gets their share
It's the same for you and me,
It never makes distinctions
And its rays of heat are free.

Yes, there's a feeling of elation
When the warmth comes from the sun,
It leaves us feeling better
When another day is done.

So roll on in the summer time
When the sky is cloudless blue,
And welcome in the sunshine
As it burns the skin off you.

EF, May 2009.

Spade Calling

Jimmy called a spade a spade,
He filtered nothing down,
He would say it as he saw it
And he wouldn't even frown,
"If you don't like it, you can lump it",
He would say, composed and cool,
"I won't make myself a hypocrite
And I'll be nobody's fool".

Well, he never beat about the bush
Or thought for very long,
The things he said were unrehearsed,
His opinions they were strong,
He would never hurt your feelings
'Cause he claimed they were your own,
So he was not responsible
If he cut you to the bone.

But he didn't always like it
When the pendulum it swung,
And he couldn't always take it
From someone else's tongue,
So in time he learned that silence
Was the medicine for his sins,
It was best to keep his mouth shut
Or to take it on the chin.

EF, June 2009.

Air France

"Unimaginable" is the only word
To describe my feelings strong,
To be sitting on board that Air France Plane
When the whole dammed thing went wrong,
Then go through all the motions
Of safety belts and storms
And deal with all the turbulence,
As well as being informed.

"Horrific" are the thoughts in mind
Of knowing what's in store,
But one can only speculate
Who prayed? Who yelled? Who swore?
Did it drop like a stone to the ocean?
Did it land on the sea like a swan?
How many were the cries of terror?
Was it seconds before they were gone?

Will anyone ever be certain
What happened on that fatal night?
Two hundred and twenty eight people
Four-Four-Seven, the name of that flight,
It was flying from Rio to Paris
And it left on the last day in May,
The danger no one could have known
When passengers and plane flew away.

EF, 4th June 2009.

Worry

Worry, Worry, Worry,
It's the worst thing we can do,
It's like interest paid on trouble
Before it's even due,
It's like trying to solve a problem
Before it raised its head,
It's like looking round a corner
When the road is straight ahead.

Worry, Worry, Worry,
Is just a useless waste of time,
It's like looking for a mountain
Every day to try and climb,
It's like looking for a valley
To fill with all your tears,
Wishing, wishing, wishing,
You could turn back all the years.

Worry, Worry, Worry,
Is not worth an ounce of space,
There'll be time enough for sorrow
When our troubles we embrace,
So if you're looking for a milestone
To entangle round your neck,
Then worry, hurry, worry,
You'll end up a nervous wreck.

EF, June 2009.

The Way to Hell

The road to hell is paved with good intentions
With people always saying what they'll do,
With all-aspiring plans I have to mention,
But never actually seeing any through.

For some when asked will say, "It's not a problem,
I will do that right away for you, I will",
But after many days and weeks of waiting
The promises they made are empty still.

Now saying yes, can be an easy option,
"Just relax and I will sort it out for you",
Sometimes for them it simply doesn't matter
They pen your name and shove you in the queue.

For hell is piled up full with good intentions
They will serve to put a smile on Satan's face,
For he knows it always helps to make us angry
When people tell us lies is commonplace.

So commit yourself with simple wee agreements
And see them through the best way that you can,
And don't go making any false impressions
It will leave you feeling much the better man.

EF, June 2009.

Banbridge

I don't go to the town much now,
With their traffic lights and wardens,
The whole thing is too stressful,
And severe on all your organs.

For it used to be five minutes,
Gathered up your odds and ends,
You could nip in quick and out again,
With time to greet a friend.

But now you sit and watch the red,
For they never seem to change,
With no-one going anywhere
The town seems out of range.

You can't stop here and you can't stop there,
Or you're liable to get a fine,
So I simply can't be bothered now
All the offers I decline.

So if you are going into Banbridge town,
Give yourself at least an hour,
Then you will not return out home,
With your insides feeling sour.

EF, June 2009.

A Victim

Oh dark, oh darkest memories,
Black monsters come to mind,
I recognise them, all of them,
The years I left behind.

But every now and then for me
Those memories take their toll,
They took my heart, they took my youth,
They tried to take my soul.

And down the years they rested
Those memories planted deep,
The tears I wept avoided them
From waking from their sleep.

But now it has been opened
This box of evil deeds
The world now knows
What happened us
The pangs of guilt are freed.

For we were not responsible
Our innocence was so pure,
To think how they abused us
How they used us all like whores.

Are they haunted by their silence?
Are they muzzled by their sins?
When they finally face their maker
Will they reluctantly give in?

EF, June 2009.

99

The Troubles 1969

The road was like a jungle
That resembled human trees,
Filled with soldiers,
dressed in army green,
Spread round like honey bees,

They were closing off the side streets
Using barrels and sheets of tin,
There was barbed wire
Stretched like fiddle strings
There was racket, there was din.

And I was in the middle
Heading down that Springfield Road,
I had just escaped from Mackies
Woodvale factories stringent code,
I remember all the buses red
They were forced to stand there still,
For me it was much quicker,
Walking fast would fit the bill.

Insanity surrounded me
On down the Grosvenor Road,
Manoeuvring on motorbikes
Men fled as headlights glowed,
There was dust and dirt
On peoples shirts,
There was horns and sirens blare,
In silent shock and terror
I could only stop and stare.

EF, June 2009.

Time for Someone

Sometimes it's very difficult
To spread yourself around,
There's a lot of people waiting
Fingers pointing to the ground,
Demands can seem unending
With so many things to do
And at times it is impossible
To get round to you and you.

For I cannot split myself in two
There is only one of me,
And I only have so many hours
To share with actively,
As well as that I need a break
Sometimes to shower my head,
So I'm going to have to step away
My love I cannot spread.

But I will make a conscious effort
In between to share my love,
I will try to be there just for you
With God's help from above,
So don't be hard on me today
For I'm trying to do my best,
I will make a little time for you,
Just get it off your chest.

EF, June 2009.

Kidney Stone

I am laying here tonight in bed
As sick as I can be,
I've been up to the toilet Lord
And I cannot even pee,
I know I'm not the greatest
When it comes to tholing pain,
But this is a really nasty one
You'll agree, I must complain.

I've never had this thing before
It stings and aches like mad,
When I think in all comparison
It's the worst I've ever had,
It resembles a bad toothache
With a heartbeat deep inside,
In fact it's just intolerable
The truth I cannot hide.

Well it came on all so sudden
And it wakened me from sleep,
I rushed up to the toilet but the pain just made me weep,
I crawled around the vinyl floor
Upon my hands and knees,
To try and bring me some relief that I at least could pee,
But it was all in vain, the pain
Just kept on getting worse,
I'm going to have to pray for time, let nature take its course,
For I could never sum it up in this short little verse,
The pain of one wee kidney stone, in its journey to disperse.
But the doctor gave me tablets now
They have brought me some relief,
I pray the Lord to spare me 'ere
From any further grief. E.F. June 2009

Unfair Killing

Is it fair to kill a hare,
by greyhound or by gun?
Is it right to kill a snipe
For pleasure or for fun?

Do you blame for shooting game
The farmer and his dogs?
Do you try to stop the hawks,
In the bog from catching frogs?

Well what about the lions
In the wilds out hunting deer?
Well what about the vultures
Stripping bones when death appears?

Can we justify the abattoirs?
Where they slaughter all the lambs?
Can we vindicate the massacre
That took place in Vietnam?

Now if we can eat a piece of meat
Or condone the latest war,
Then maybe it is true to say
The above we don't abhor,
For in the acts of killing
There are similar patterns flow,
The animals, they are animals
But do human beings "know"?

EF, June 2009.

The Biggest Waste

"The biggest waste in the West is water",
Mother Teresa used these words,
The problem is for most of us
The words just go unheard,
When the rain is falling heavy
And is flowing down the streams,
We're all inclined to think of it,
As plenty in extremes.

And maybe that is very true
When downpours leave the sky,
Many people living here
Could scream sometimes and cry,
For we run around complaining
That it's always, always raining,
But it only takes a day or two
To dry the drops remaining.

And so the ground it withers
All the taps are barred from use,
The Spelga Dam is dropping
And a ban is introduced,
It's then we realise the waste
By father, son and daughter,
When we wash the car
And wash the yard
With lovely drinking water.

EF, June 2009.

Sweetheart Dreams

We met one night
When the sky was bright
And the moon was shining down,
She paused for a while
With a beautiful smile
As she stood in her evening gown.

From far and near
They were gathered here
All dressed up for the ball,
The fertile rich
And the way in which
They stood, displaying all.

They had bands of gold
Around their necks,
Their fingers and their wrists,
Entwined with pearls and diamonds,
Figures slim and chauvinist,
Champagne moisture on their lips
And lipstick red as wine,
Trying, each one, to move gracefully
Modelling a different design.

But my eyes were fixed on this one:
She was beautiful from within,
The wealth she wore and the riches stored
Were all beneath her skin.

EF, June 2009.

Be Careful

There is one thing in all our lives
That we should not forget,
For it may be just the case for us
At times, when our minds are set,
That what we do, or what we say,
Should not be set in stone,
For we may have to eat our words,
Our principles all disown.

You see, this life is very strange
And it has many ups and downs,
Indeed what often goes around
Can sometimes come around,
If you should blemish a person's name
For the sake of scandal spread,
Then someday you may find the same
Is propped upon your head.

So just be careful what you say
Be attentive to what you do,
For you never know the moment
It could all return to you,
You see there is this saying
'What goes round will come round',
So be mindful in your giving,
For some day, it could rebound.

EF, June 2009.

Too Busy To Call

You would maybe see him once or twice
Over the course of a year,
Although he lived just up the way
His voice you would seldom hear,
For he didn't wander very far
And he'd hobble from limb to limb,
We could pass his house in silence,
But we were there to bury him.

I'm sure there were times he was lonely
And would have needed a bit of craic,
But the days and the hours are very short
When you're carrying the world on your back,
He had the knowledge of any computer.
Experience, he was full to the brim,
We couldn't get a minute to listen,
But we were there to bury him.

"God, he was a great oul character",
"He was surely one of a kind",
Just two of the comments bespoken
Whilst following the coffin behind,
But talking is wasted on dead ears
For life it had ended for Tim,
We couldn't get time for him living,
But we were there to bury him.

EF, July 2009.

Marriage Advice

It was about my older sibling
When she had marriage on her mind,
The advice my father gave her
Wasn't meant to be unkind,
But he stressed, in not so many words,
The language he could find,
It was aimed in one direction
Very close to her behind.

"Now there are lots of ways to put it
But there is only one I know,
I will make no bones about it
For I heard it long ago,
If you take the time to listen
It will keep you in good stead,
So, my daughter, be attentive
To my words I hope you heed".

"You have chosen to be married
And my blessings you will hold,
I will be there to support you
In the years that I grow old".
Then I always can remember
What he said to my big sister,
"When you burn your arse, my dear,
You can sit upon the blister".

EF, July 2009.

Bed Brain

"Bed again", I must refrain
From thinking when I dream,
For without the use of paper
My head is full of reams,
It's written down in memory,
Packed in like fish in nets,
The brain is overloaded
Hoping I will not forget.

"Morning again", I can't sustain,
My head is going to burst,
It feels as though the lid is off
I think this time's the worst!
What can I say? What will I do?
Where will I go? The day has flew!
What happens next? I'm way behind!
Much more of this will wreck my mind.

"Bed again", I must abstain
From losing all this sleep,
I've just kicked into overtime,
No slot for counting sheep,
Impossible to unwind myself
I'm off again once more,
Where do I get the recipe
To turn around and snore?

EF, July 2009.

Letter Writing

My daughter, she was writing a letter one day
The contents of which, I did not have a say,
It was only when she finally came to an end
That she turned in a panic, no more she could fend.
"I can never remember", says she, "my minds poor,
What way this dammed letter is signed after Yours-
Sincerely, or Faithfully, can you say which is which?
It's driving me mental, "the son of a bitch".

Says I, "Take a deep breath, and catch yourself on
Don't get so excited, is your patience all gone?
Just think for a minute, who you're posting it to
With love and affection, or with anonymous view?
If it's someone you love, or a friend you admire
Then sincere you will be, it can never backfire,
But if it's only a line to a person unknown
Sign it just faithfully, no seeds have been sown".

Well, she turned with the pen a big sigh of relief,
"That always for me is a great source of grief,
No matter how often I rehearse past my brain
I just keep forgetting it, over and over again",
Well say's I, "Just remember who you're writing it to,
It will keep you informed of the facts if you do,
Unless it's the undertaker you wish to inform:
Sign "Yours Eventually" is the role you perform".

EF, July 2009.

The Big Country

I have travelled round this countryside,
I have watched the green grass grow,
I have strayed across the daisy fields,
And I've watched the rivers flow

I have grown up with the countryside,
I have fresh air in my genes,
I have strayed across the meadows
In my youth and through my teens.

I have always loved the countryside,
I have breathed it in my blood,
I have strayed in all directions,
Tying hay and gathering spuds.

I have always lived in the countryside,
I have memories, born and bred,
I have always been so fortunate
As I have oft' times said.

I have plans to die in the countryside,
I have dreams to end it here,
I have thought about it often
But not for a few more years,

"Please God".

EF, August 2009.

Days Gone By

Paddy was a big strong man,
His neck run down to his wrists,
He could lift a ten stone bag of spuds
And without a problem shift,
He could grape out dung in 'barrow fulls
And spread it all over his land,
He never would think of machinery
For he done all his work by hand.

He could scrape the yard from end to end
He could work from morning to night,
As big a man you would ever see
He was muscular, strong and tight,
Two eggs for breakfast, bacon and toast
He was fond of the mush-a-rooms,
Three mugs of tae he could gulp away
As happy as a flower in bloom.

Well, he never had a care or a worry
And money was never his God,
For he always believed it was better,
The simpler the life you could trod,
And that was the way that he lived it,
It's the way that he ended his days,
He said he had learned from his father
And nothing would change his old ways.

EF, August 2009.

Healthy and Normal

As normal, healthy people
We wake up to every day,
We take so much for granted
In each and every way,
For all of us have faculties
That serve us all so well
We see, we hear,
We touch, and speak,
So too, our sense of smell.

There are people live in wheel chairs,
There are those confined to bed,
There are many with no arms or legs
Just wishing they were dead,
There are people with diseases
There are those who have no hope,
There are many live in poverty
On pills and drugs and dope.

Take time then to be thankful
For to count your blessings all,
To appreciate the wonders,
Be them big or be them small.
For if you want to see a miracle
Performed in every way,
Then just look at someone healthy,
Someone normal, every day.

EF, August 2009.

Orbit

66 thousand miles an hour
This earth goes round the sun,
That's faster than a bullet
Fired from a sniper's gun.

18 miles per second
Believe this fact or not,
It's beyond our comprehension
For our minds are in a trot.

It takes one year to travel round
And the timing is Swiss made,
Its speed it never varies
As the centuries invade.

93 million miles away
Is the radius from the sun,
That's the way it's always been
Since time and earth begun.

And hopefully for all of us
Who form the human race,
It won't stop for a second
Or we'll all land up in space.

EF, August 2009.

*Please note, actually the earth travels round the sun at an average speed
of 66,600 miles per hour. That is 18.5 miles per second.

Lost In Time

'Out of sight, out of mind',
They always used to say,
'Twas relating to a person
Who was usually far away,
Now they may have emigrated
To a place across the globe,
You forget about the whereabouts
Their lives you never probe.

Well, they could be in a nursing home
That's just around the corner,
It's maybe just as far away
As joy is to a mourner,
For when you cannot see them
There's no reason to be kind,
You simply never focus:
'Out of sight is out of mind'.

Now they maybe live beside you,
One or two or three doors down,
There's rumours of their passing
When you're shopping up the town,
For it's always more important
Keeping up with worldly news,
Out of sight and out of mind
Is the state of life you choose.

EF, August 2009.

Psalm 90, Verse 10

"The years of our life are threescore and ten
Or by reason of strength fourscore"
But many are given the grace from above
which helps them to live many more.

"Yet for many their span is trouble and toil
Soon gone and we all fly away"
But that is the passage it's set out to be
We are all of us, having our day.

For some it goes quick, for some it goes slow
Yet for some it has only begun,
While many are struggling up near to the end
There are those who in years they get none.

Now all of it's way beyond our control,
Our life like a buffalo's breath,
It appears for a while in the cold, fresh air
Then disappears, right into death.

Though certain we're not of the moment,
And the day or the hour is not clear,
But certain we are of the moment,
We just never know when it is near.

EF, August 2009.

Pay Up and Shut Up

It started off and the agreement was made,
A payment in sixty days,
Well, usually you don't dispute this
If that's what the company says,
But then the boss-man calls to say
That the invoices are all wrong,
Made out to a different company
To whom he did not belong.

So the payments stalled for a little while
But he was sure he'd make it right,
The start of the lies to flow from tongues
Of people who stay out of sight,
I'm putting you through to another man
It's his job to get you paid
But after another week or so
You're still twiddling your thumbs instead.

Now there's still no money, another two months
Has passed and the bank is dry,
You couldn't believe a word that's said
From people who stall and lie,
So then they send an email
Another tactic to delay,
The last thing that they want to do
Is just cough up and pay.

From one man to another, all directors in the firm,
No one can sign a cheque for you
Like worms they twist and squirm,
Then the news comes there's a meeting
To be held next Wednesday week,
It's now another fortnight, time to buy for profits seek,
And all at our expense they fraud
With conscience free they lie,
They could not care and do not care
As to whether you live or die.

EF, August 2009.

Faith Fool

Have you got in touch with Jesus or not,
In all your years of prayer?
Are you totally convinced that God exists,
Or do you think that there's nobody there?

How do you know when you turn to Him,
That you're not just fooling yourself?
Do you really believe when you pray every day
In a God who gives you your health?

When you're faced with a serious problem
And you turn to God in prayer,
Do you sometimes hear between your ears,
A voice that says, "I don't care"?

Well, I'm sure there's a Thomas in everyone
That's lurking somewhere in your head,
No hope of removing that mountain,
In truth, sure enough has been said.

So try to be truthful and honest
And throw all your pride to the ground,
In a life that is moving so swiftly
Is there someone you still haven't found?

EF, August 2009.

The Loafer

Larry was a loafer, laziness was his state,
Rising in the mornings was his daily hate,
Washing dirty dishes, lifting filthy clothes,
Larry was as useless as the shabby beard he grows.

Larry was a loafer when he was at his work,
Taking three steps backwards was a daily shirk,
Always letting others do chores for him as well,
Hanging round in waiting, for the boss to ring the bell.

Larry was a loafer, in and out of love,
He offered no commitment when he found a dove,
Always said relationships weren't his cup of tea
Larry was too busy looking after 'me'.

Larry was a loafer and his life was passing by,
He often spent the evenings looking at the sky,
One day passed another, he wasn't too concerned,
Never get excited sure there's nothing more to learn.

Larry was a loafer all his days they were the same,
He never made an effort so he never was in pain,
Things like being courteous, brave or even gallant,
It never meant a thing to him, for he never used his talents.

EF, August 2009.

Thanks, Mary

You made your presence known Mary
With this picture of my Mum,
As soon as I sat eyes on it
I was totally overcome.

For you kept it safe for sixty years
It has now returned to me,
You give me back my mother's youth
For my family all to see.

And then you sent your letters
To describe you both as friends,
How she left you with her picture
When the work came to an end.

It travelled far across the sea
And you kept it from being lost,
This little piece of treasure
Who could estimate its cost?

I will always keep it, Mary,
For it's worth its weight in gold,
It will remind me of the friend she had
In the Hazelbank of old.

EF, August 2009.

Time Run Out

Do you ever think of your own shelf-life?
What you'll do when your date expires?
For it doesn't always work
The way you might think,
Or turn out to your hearts desires.

For things have a habit of changing to sour
When you're sitting on the shelf for so long,
You spend your whole life
Doing the things that you like,
Then suddenly, you don't even belong.

Being youthful and mobile, the pitfalls are few,
And it's hard to envisage the day,
When the freedom of living
In a house of your own,
Is exchanged for a nursing home stay.

Well, sometimes it can not be avoided,
Sometimes it's the only way out,
But for someone who's used
To the freedom of life,
The shock can kill them outright.

So when do you think you'll be 'best-before'?
What date do think you'll outlast?
And when it arrives will you be prepared
To fit in the mould when it's cast?

EF, September 2009.

No Guarantees

When you start out on a journey,
Any journey,
You will enter the unknown,
Even though you're always sure
For certain
Where you're going.

For you can never tell the day,
The minute or the hour,
When everything can go astray,
It is not within your power.

When you plan your route,
The highway,
Put in place the highway code,
And at no time take for granted
Who you meet
When on the road.

For you can never tell the moment,
In an instant or a flash,
When everything could crumble
You could have a terrible crash,
You may be doing all things right
Completely in control,
When suddenly out of nowhere
Some poor idiot takes a roll.

When you start out on a journey,
Any journey,
Always remember 'No Guarantees'.

EF, September 2009.

Follow Old Footsteps

Sit down and put your boots on,
Take a stroll through Banbridge town,
Give yourself an hour or two
And dander up and down,
Consider those before you
In your memory you will find,
Look down upon the pavement
At the prints they left behind.

Then consider very carefully
As you thread the paths they trod,
How it was for them before you,
When you meet someone and nod,
For they counted up their pennies
Just enough to spend on bread,
There were rarely any extras,
Just enough to keep them fed.

Then put yourself in their shoes
And pause for a little while,
And ask yourself the question
As you walk with them a mile,
Are we living any different?
Or are we any better off?
For our progress and possessions
Can we look to them and scoff?

For now we have the money
And we all can have enough,
But if we were fairly honest
Living life is still as tough.

EF, September 2009.

What's Done is Done!

Some things better left undone,
Some better left unsaid,
Whilst you could argue all the same
That it would clear your head,
Sometimes just leave well alone
More said the less the better,
Unless of course you want to cause
A bitter, deep vendetta.

Someone will always make the point
Some things are better said,
That you will know just where you stand,
Put everything to bed,
Some day you'll get it off your back
And you'll lay it on the line,
You're going to make it loud and clear
That you are not the swine.

Some ways are surly not the best,
Some words might clear the air,
But don't be tempted any time
To fall into that snare,
For being right can cause a fight
That you will surly rue,
The one that will be hurt the most
Guarantee it could be you.

EF, September 2009.

Unleash

Don't bother to look over your shoulder,
Don't focus on what's in the past,
You can not remove the ingredients
Whenever the die it is cast.

There is much to endure in the present,
Each day brings its own kind of hell,
The burdens of life can be difficult,
Take yesterdays and bid them farewell.

Sometimes you can dream about living,
Of changing your life and your job,
In a future that's always uncertain
You are carried along with the mob.

Don't bother to dwell on what's over,
Don't cry over milk that is spilled,
Twist your head round from your shoulder
And walk in a body that's drilled.

Don't climb up hills 'til you get there,
Don't fly 'til your wings are in bloom,
Give yourself space for the moment,
Try not to encounter the gloom.

Do not take a hold of the nettle,
Unless you intend to grasp tight,
Just place yourself into the present
And sleep like a baby tonight.

EF, September 2009.

Mind Blank

You get away from writing poems,
I haven't done it for a while,
But today I'll make an effort
I'm going to walk that extra mile,
Good ideas they will pass me,
If I don't sit down and write,
I will now take up the mantle
The bullet I will bite.

So I'm going to endeavour
Just to show a small amount,
And it will not be essential
To inscribe a full account,
But the urge in me is pining,
To create and pen a verse,
Yet it seems I'm out of practice
I will have to call rehearse.

But the bottle, it is empty,
As I turn it upside down,
For I cannot find a sentence,
Not a verb and not a noun,
So the writing it is over
Well at least now for today,
I will have to scrap the mantle
And just throw the pen away.

EF, September 2009.

126

Me and Only Me

Caring what people do today
Is of no concern to me,
How they choose to spend their time
We all might disagree,
For each has ways of going mad
And so to each his own,
Many choose to roam the world
While others stay at home.

For I am not responsible
How others live their life,
Whether they stay single
Or take themselves a wife,
And I am not responsible
For all the things they say,
Maybe criticise the neighbours
Could be all they do today.

But I should have this deep concern
Of things that I can change,
And the first on my agenda
Is within my shooting range,
For standing right beside me
And behind me and within,
Is the person with the mastery
To change the world we're in.

EF, September 2009.

Loneliness

Tonight as I sit here alone in my chair,
I was happy your presence a while for to share,
For sadness and sorrow were close to my mind,
When all of a sudden I felt in my prime,
You knocked and you called
And you opened my door,
I could feel all my burdens
Disappear through the floor.

Well, you told me a story
And you sang me song,
And I was so happy
I just sang along,
For rare is the chance now
And my friends they are few,
Bear with me in patience
While I talk to you.

You know there's a saying
When loneliness reigns,
That laughing and singing
Will dampen the pain,
It's hard to describe it
The times I have cried,
So thank you for calling
To be by my side.

EF, September 2009.

After Life

I'm not sure if I fear death
Or just the time of death,
For I know sooner or later
We all draw final breath.

But true to you I sayeth
I'm not sure if I fear death,
Or think about the dayeth
When beneath the clay I layeth.

I'm not sure if I fear dying
Or just the way of dying,
To say that I don't care too much
I think I would be lying.

But true to you I'm trying
Not to think too much of dying,
So I'm opting out of saying
When beneath the soil I'm laying.

So death I can't be sure of
And of dying I'm not so sure,
So I think I'll just postpone this
'Cause it all sounds immature.

EF, September 2009.

Guardian

I heard an old voice say one day
That the dead could see us all,
So to watch your step, be careful
How you thread and not to fall,
For they were in a spirit world
As was their eyes and ears,
So be mindful of your errors,
And to recognise your fears.

For they could see what we could see
As plain as light of day,
Every movement they were watching
Even when we went astray,
They surround us like a shadow
Hover over like a dove,
Guide us in the right direction
And inspire us all in love.

They've been called our guardian angels
Helping us to pave the way,
Even though they weren't invited
Their intention is to stay,
So be careful who you speak of
And the words you choose to use,
Make a list of all your actions
It's for sure you cannot lose.

EF, September 2009.

One Good Turn

If you're going to do a good turn,
Then it won't be done in vain,
But always bear in mind though
You'll have some amount of pain,
For to do the slightest favour
For a friend who is in need,
It is sure to give you hassle
In your efforts to succeed.

There's this word 'appreciation',
Which will often spring to mind,
Sometimes it's not forthcoming
And your friends can seem unkind,
But you always should remember
What you do is what you do,
Do not make them feel indebted,
It will be the strength of you.

If you're going to do a good turn,
Then approach it with your heart,
If there's the slightest other motive
Then you should not even start,
Do not raise your expectations,
Do not wish for something back,
Eaten bread is soon forgotten
So just do it for the craic.

EF, September 2009.

James

I remember his face
When he worked round our place
He always afforded a smile,
He seemingly wasn't so bothered
By much, prepared to go that extra mile.

He was always on time
With the eight o'clock chime,
He was humble and gentle and strong,
His body was silent except for the times
When he calmly was humming a song.

He never would ask
What would be his next task,
Intelligence was part of his frame,
Common sense would prevail,
Through the work he would sail
He was always on top of his game.

Well, over the years
He would tackle his fears
When something, a challenge, was set,
He was never afraid of the progress he made
Saying, "Meet it and have no regrets".

Well, that was his cast,
Obliging and fast,
He could tackle almost anything,
But alas brings a tear
With his presence not here
His absence brought on by death's sting.

EF, 3rd September 2009.

Partners in Fur

Whilst walking down the footpath
In the early morning air,
I was suddenly confronted
By a rabbit and a hare,
They stopped a hundred yards from me
With hind legs propped in place,
No attempt was made to panic
As they stared me face to face.

I could not understand this
'Twas a sight I'd never seen,
When swiftly there before me
They formed a gap between,
And one of them invited me
To take a step and stand,
And reaching out their paws to me
They put them in my hands.

Totally I was blew away,
Their eyes were full of tears,
They said that they were ladies
Trapped in fur for years,
And I was still in total shock
My inside it was screaming,
When suddenly the clock went off
"Oh God, I'm only dreaming!"

EF, September 2009.

The Good Times Are Over

They're paying off a hundred here,
A hundred people there,
Shops are closing on the high streets,
Factories shutting everywhere,
There is massive unemployment
And production it has slowed,
More pressure on the taxpayer
To spread this heavy load.

Employers they are cutting down
To try and ease the bills,
With no demand for anything
It could drive you to the hills,
For there's many people worried sick
Never unemployed before,
They simply don't know what to do
To face this dinosaur.

We all knew that this was coming
But maybe not so quick,
It seemed to happen overnight,
Backfiring like an oul mule's kick,
Now how long the presents going to last
Or in the end who will survive,
For the news it just gets bleaker
The climb down has arrived.

But really if you stop and think
Of what's been going on,
The whole damn thing was stupid
It was like a marathon,
For buying, buying, buying
It was peoples' middle names
We were all in together
Like wee children playing games.

EF, September 2009.

Martina and Gareth

If the two of you can always be as happy as today,
With confidence, enough to grow and change along the way,
If you can keep your love so deep, like today as man and wife,
You will find the time to share your joy
With others in your life.

If you can walk together, through your marriage hand in hand,
Yet still support the goals and dreams
That each of you has planned,
If you can dare to always share
Your separate ways together,
Then all the joys of this today
Will stay with you forever.

Ponder in your hearts today, the plans that you have made,
Remind each other constantly and do not let them fade,
Relive the dreams that each of you have seen this day come true,
Keep them close and cherish them, the things you say and do.

Surround yourselves with memories
Of the happy times you've known,
Caring, understanding times, and the way that you have grown,
Treasure always all these things, they are such a special part,
Your union here with the one you love, always in your heart.

And don't forget as time goes on to share a little faith
If God is walking with you then your marriage will be safe,
For the modern world will test you, trials will come your way
Just remember Gareth and Martina,
"Love each other every day".

EF, 30th October 2010. Written for my daughter's wedding.

Commitments

Jesus Lord, I commit my life,
I commit my life to You,
Help me Lord to balance that
With the work I have to do,
For I have obligations Lord
To try and pay my bills,
So the life I live for You, oh Lord,
Can quickly go downhill.

But still I have this duty Lord
My allegiance to fulfil,
It's not that You're are forcing me
To execute Your will,
But in between my wanting to
And needing You as well,
There's all the worldly pressures
That I'm trying to expel.

So stay with me today Lord
As I evaluate my plans,
If I should fall from grace Lord
May it be into Your hands,
For this is what I want now
To know that You are near,
Commit my life to You Lord
I hope I've made that clear.

EF, October 2009.

Matrimony

If we spent more time together
We could face all kinds of weather,
If we ponder on our vows
We can save all kinds of rows,
If we put each other first
Then for love we'll never thrist,
If we give to one another
Then we will elevate each other,
If we look for all the good
We will change each others mood,
If we raise ourselves and praise
Then all hurt we will erase,
If we reach out full of care
It will be our greatest prayer.

If we spend less time together
We let go of each ones tether,
To forget your wedding vows
You'll forget your wedding spouse,
If we put each other last
Then the shine will fade off fast,
If we never learn to give
Then we don't know how to live,
If our failures greet us first
Then we must expect the worst,
If we don't take time to praise
Then we'll lose the good old days,
If our hearts are not on fire
Then we've lost our hearts desires.

EF, October 2009.

The Ladder

There is something I will share with you
It's a very urgent matter,
Concerning everyone of you
Who choose to use a ladder,
Take care how you position it
The slope, the slant, the rake,
Be careful when you're using it
With every step you take.

And don't get too familiar,
Always pause and always stop,
For a ladder never slips until
You're standing at the top,
And then without a warning
When you're stretching past your span,
It can only take a second,
You will be a sorry man.

Now a ladder is a useful tool,
It serves in many ways,
It makes our lives much easier
But the rules you must obey,
So get someone to hold the thing
When you're reaching for the sky,
The risk will not be worth it
If you prematurely die.

EF, October 2009.

Time Once Again

You can almost measure the length of a week
By the casual wink of an eye,
The lid it has hardly went up and down twice
'Til the week it has passed you by.

You can almost compare the speed of time
With a thought that comes into your head,
It comes and it goes as quick as a flash
It's in the past as soon as it's said.

So you have to meet the thing head on
For it's not just as bad as it seems,
If you make the most of the time you have got
You're sure to fulfil all you dreams.

Don't sit around waiting 'til daylight,
Don't lie about waiting for dark,
Don't crouch in the corner a hermit
Or the cobwebs upon you will park.

There is time if you get up and do it
Each day it has twenty four hours,
There is no-one can do the thing for you
It is you have been given the power.

So forget about how the time passes
The present is all we have got,
Don't focus on all the tomorrows
For seeing them, sure you may not.

EF, October 2009.

Hair Loss

I couldn't bear to loose my hair
Or to watch it disappear,
The reason is you see of course
I've had it now for years.

It was always very curly
And the roots were darkish red,
I liked to keep it nice and long
Like a well maned thoroughbred.

My nickname was a 'Ginger Bap',
They called me this at school,
But it never really bothered me
And I always kept my cool.

Sometimes I meet the 'slagers'
With their bald and shiny tops,
I run my fingers through my hair
To let them see my mop.

It's my turn now for slating
As our heads we all compare,
When it comes to match the thatching
I can say that mines still there.

They can't give me the nickname
For our schooldays are all gone,
But unfortunately the 'Ginger Bap'
Goes back to "Once upon…".

EF, October 2009.

Give to Get

Why is it those who do the least
Are the ones who expect the most?
Why is it those who are last to move
Are always the first to boast?

Why are those who never do work
Will always expect to be paid?
Why is it those who never take part
Are always the worst to persuade?

Why are those who don't pay a stamp
Will always expect the best care?
Why is it those who never go out
Will give out when there's nobody there?

Why is it those who don't earn a wage
Are the ones who never pay tax?
Why is it they are the very same ones
Who always have the time to relax?

Why is it those who are always receiving
Just never take part in the giving?
Why is it they are totally convinced
That the country owes them a living?

EF, October 2009.

Spotless Me

Now all of us can give and take
And exceptions we can make,
Forgiveness fills up all our hearts
When a livelihood's at stake,
For none of us are spotless
And mistakes will come what may,
Events that come to haunt us
Each and every single day.

Now forgiveness it will travel far
And boundaries it will break,
After all we're only human
So we'll grieve for others sake,
We will not allow misfortune
When it visits some poor soul,
To create or plant a hardness
In our hearts we take control.

But there's times when that's not easy
And it is in this present day,
It just goes beyond acquittal
When you hear of peoples pay,
For they get enormous wages
And expenses all through in,
And still they sponge the system
What we've seen is one big sin.

EF, October 2009.

Smoking Ban

Smoking it is banned now, in all hotels and clubs,
You're not allowed to drag a fag in any bar or pub,
You would not find an ashtray anywhere in sight,
Banning all the stinking butts, many say was right.

For some were inconsiderate, smoking in your face,
Even in a restaurant, which was totally out of place,
No concern for others, the smoke went up your nose
Morning, noon and later the stench was on your clothes.

Now many people could not wait, when even at a meal
A fag between their fingers, made you want to squeal,
Your eyes began to water; tears would fill the plate,
All the evil in your mind for them would contemplate.

And so in public places there's a ban on cigarettes
For most the population it's a ban without regrets,
Yes, eating out's a pleasure, no tobacco to inhale
You can even sit in comfort now and sip a glass of ale.

For smoking it is filthy, the restrictions here to stay
With all the reinforcing it will mean you must obey,
When you're sitting in a restaurant, a café or a pub
You'll need to find another way to occupy your gub.

But don't get too excited, there's pollution on the street,
People stand in doorways dumping fag ends at your feet,
The footpath is an ashtray, you need to hold your breath
Be careful when out walking, for you could catch a death.

EF, October 2009.

The Mystery Woman

I heard this knock upon my door; the night was dark and cold,
Upon opening it so slowly, stood a woman grey and old,
She said her name was Mary, 'twas by chance she passed my way,
And asked if it would be alright, for an hour or two to stay.

I said, "Come in, take off your coat and sit beside the fire,
Tell me where you've journeyed from, I'm sure you must be tired,
Your face is not familiar, I don't think we've ever met",
For strangely something tells me, that I would not forget.

"Well now", she said, "You're far too young, you'd not remember me,
For I was born too many years before you came to be,
I don't know how I got here, and I don't know where I've been,
But it always seems to happen me, when it comes to Halloween."

"I knock a time or two on doors, yes, maybe once or twice,
But no one seems to answer them, and I know that is their choice,
For everyone is busy now, and there's noise in every room,
It's almost like they're living in a modern ancient tomb."

"There's news from all around the world to occupy your time,
It's sad to think of wasted hours, from people in their prime,
They follow soaps and serials, and weekly programmes too,
It seems an awful pity, when there's so much work to do."

"There's a simple explanation why I'm sitting here tonight,
So forgive me if I startled you, or filled you up with fright,
You heard me when I knocked; you opened up and let me in,
And shared a little time with me and let me warm my skin."

Then up she got, no more was said, she quickly left the fire,
I couldn't help but ask her, had she someplace to retire,
But not a word was uttered as she stepped out through the door,
I haven't seen this woman since, not after or before.

EF, October 2009.

Remember This

Don't forget all your achievements
During the times when you are down,
Just remember them especially
When your sorrows you might drown,
For inclined to just forget them
You might be, when things are bad,
But for God's sake just remember
All the good times you have had.

Think of one thing you've accomplished
In your lifetime up to now,
Close your eyes and turn your mind back
It will all return somehow,
Do not beat yourself no further
Break the stick that leaves you sore,
Promise God and all around you
You won't punish you no more.

Make a list of all your good deeds
Try hard not to be surprised,
You will find the list is bigger
Than you'd have ever realised,
For the years can make you bitter
You could flog yourself to death,
Just remember that God loves you
So love yourself in every breath.

EF, October 2009.

Mammy, Mammy, Mammy

Men will never understand the way that women are made,
When it comes to the everyday things in life
The women are never afraid,
They take on more and more and more
With the children's needs up front,
Their ages makes no difference:
Mammy's there to take the brunt.

They nurse them when they're babies
They cry with them to school,
Sometimes you'd think the baby's knew that mummy was their fool,
They cuddle them and kiss them saying, "Who's a lovely boy",
With daddy thinking all the time
'She's playing with her toy'.

They spoil them with their giving, fulfilling all their needs,
When all the time in daddy's head
She's sowing the wrong seeds,
"For God's sake let them walk my dear
They're big and overgrown,
No need for you to carry them
They've two legs of their own".

But mammy's having none of it, and she says, "Sure I don't mind,
It's the least that I can do for them; sure it helps me to unwind",
She makes their beds, she washes clothes,
And she irons, bakes and cooks,
They get hand-in-hand attention, like a prison full of crooks.

Now Daddy cannot understand what makes his poor wife tick,
For she is so preoccupied smothering all her chicks,
For when it comes to instincts they are mostly all maternal,
The kids would not be spoiled as much
If the instincts were paternal.

EF, October 2009.

Frances

You're abroad but not forgotten
In New Zealand far away,
We think about you often,
Yes, your name came up today.

For you spent some time at our house
When parties were the norm,
When all of you were children
You and Gerard were closely born.

Always gentle in your nature
You were pleasant in your smile,
And all the time considerate
When you played around awhile.

We have captured you on video
We have pictures of your face,
Playing around with our ones,
Full of innocence and grace.

Now it's fair to say we miss you
But we wish you much success,
In the life that you have chosen,
Frances, every happiness.

EF, October 2010.

The Iveagh 1970s

We used to go to the picture house every Saturday night,
It was called the Iveagh Cinema, lit up and shining bright,
Down at the bottom of Reilly Street, Patrons queued for hours,
You would cuddle to your girlfriend, to brave the windy showers.
Back then it was a novelty and it came round once a week,
We all would wait there patiently, each with tongue in cheek,
For the doors they never opened up before the time was right,
When the queue it started moving it was a very pleasing sight.

Two tickets for the balcony, that's where we liked to perch,
We would fondle up together, there was room enough to lurch,
Sometimes we'd watch the film for it was hard to split a kiss,
But in between the gasps for breath some bits we didn't miss,
Well, every now and then there'd be a thriller on the screen,
So the kissing and the courting would just be off the scene,
We would all be sitting mesmerised with the film 'Madame X',
Sure you wouldn't even dare to breathe, never mind relax.

But soon it all was over we would make our way downstairs,
And we'd talk about the picture show heading out in pairs,
The trailer on the wall it meant you could not go astray,
Of course we had to view and see what's on in seven days.
So up the street to Fuscos we would go for fish and chips,
The largest glass of Fanta was enjoyed between our lips,
Then off to have that goodnight kiss, and wait to get the bus,
Out the road with all the mates and the pictures we'd discuss.

We used to go to Banbridge town every Saturday night,
The thoughts of all the Westerns left our hearts in flight,
Waiting it was sluggish and the days were long drawn out,
But patience was rewarded for it always came about.

EF, November 2009.

Shank's Mare

Nobody walks now anymore,
They called it 'Shank's Mare',
The cheapest form of transport
It would get you anywhere,
We used to walk to shops in town
We'd walk to Sunday prayers,
We even walked it into school,
Our voices all were shared.

Nobody walks now anymore
There is one in every car,
All piled up behind the other
Not getting very far,
Sitting parked for hours on end
Stuck when the green turns red,
We spend more time at traffic lights
Than we do tucked up in bed.

Nobody walks now anymore
It's a sight that's very rare,
Sometimes an older person
Will decide on Shank's Mare,
For most of us it's far too slow
We would all arrive too late,
We're all in one big hurry
To get by our sell-by-date.

EF, November 2009.

Strangers in Common

It's amazing when you meet someone
Whom you haven't met before,
For you're not sure what to say to them
And you don't know what's in store,
Both of you are backward, both of you are shy,
Afraid you'll say the wrong things
But you know you'll have to try.

It may be at a wedding or a function of some sort,
Responses will be needed
To prepare from some retort,
And although you feeling awkward
You must make the effort still,
You may have to dig down deep
For conversation skills.

Soon you realise
They're not as backward as they seem,
They start to talk and tell you things
And they break all self esteem,
And very soon you can't believe
You have only met a while,
For now you're sharing every thing
As common as a smile.

EF, November 2009.

Ask the Lord

I'm not asking you for money Lord
And I'm not asking you for fame,
I'm not asking you for riches,
But I'm still asking all the same.

I'm not asking you for favours Lord
And I'm not asking for esteem,
I'm not asking for indulgence
But I'm still asking it would seem.

I'm not asking you for success Lord
And I'm not asking you for luck,
I'm not asking for prosperity
But I'm still asking, here I'm stuck.

I'm not asking you for health Lord
And I'm not asking you for strength,
I'm not asking for constitution
But I'm still asking you at length.

I'm not asking for long life Lord
And I'm not asking you for spirit,
I'm not asking for forgiveness
But I'm still asking to inherit.

And so it is I'm always asking
Even though I think I'm not,
When it comes to God in Heaven
This wee soul is not forgot.

EF, November 2009.

The Souls of Ballyvarley

To the souls of Ballyvarley,
May they rest in peace with God,
And to all the generations
Who lie long beneath the sod,
To the names of all my neighbours
And to those I never met,
May they join to meet their maker
In his favour pay their debts.

To the souls of Ballyvarley,
Who lived from the earthly soil,
To all of them those women and men
We share their patient toil,
We join with them in waiting
'Til in turn we shake the ghost,
No God will ask the question
Which of us has left the most.

To the souls of Ballyvarley,
Who in turn have held the fort,
You came in and out with nothing
Knowing life was very short,
But you left us all with values
More important than our wealth,
The love of friends and family
A community rich with health.

EF, 22nd November 2009.

Fly Sucker

Just be careful not to suck
When you go to "Shoo" a fly,
For it could end up in your tummy
Passing through you by and by,
It will not be very pleasant
When you come to realise,
In the horror of the moment
You have swallowed up a fly.

Now it can happen very easily
When you head out for a walk,
Just be careful with your company
If you're both inclined to talk,
For it's nasty when it happens
When a fly goes down your throat,
You just need to keep your head down
And recall these words I've wrote.

But don't worry if it happens,
Tell yourself it's not the end,
Just give it all an hour or two
And the time will make amends,
For a fly is not a filling thing
And your stomach won't feel full,
Just allow the course of nature
To secure the poor fly's cull.

And in future you be careful
When you go to "Shoo" a fly,
And be careful when you're talking
There are simple rules apply,
Blow a little harder and talk a little less
And then you won't be sorry,
For you won't be in this mess.

EF, November 2009.

153

No More Fat Cats

In all the years that I have lived my memory can't recall,
An economic doom and gloom that faces one and all,
For once it seemed, or so it seemed,
The good times they would last,
But now with pain and anguish
It would seem that they have passed.
"We're in a big recession", all the experts they have warned,
We have to tighten up our belts for the banks are overdrawn,
They've lent out all their monies, and they gave it to the rich,
Expecting that their profits would enlarge without a hitch.

But like an ancient motorbike, their plans have all backfired,
The grassroots were forgot about to name the first time buyers,
Investors spent the money erecting apartments to the sky,
Yet none of it could make sense to the ordinary passer by.
It built up like a deck of cards where was it going to end,
No limits to the massive sums the banks were going to lend,
The rich they just got richer, spending other peoples cash,
The sharks who lent the money set the course for one big crash.

And so it is and here we are, being told to knuckle down,
The governments bailing out the banks led up by Gordon Brown,
To the tune of fifty billion plus or minus one or two,
Taken from the coughers up, tax payers me and you.
And when the money is all spent to sub their bonus claims,
There'll be no work for anyone they'll leave us all in chains,
For it would be impossible to predict the futures ways.
But all of us acknowledge now, we're in for painful days.

The changes must be radical, top earners must get less,
There've overpaid themselves enough, sure anyone could guess,
The figures simply don't add up when some they get too much,
It's time to take the foot off from the gas onto the clutch.
Five hundred thousand pounds a year, that's forty grand a month,
For doing what I ask you, sure they're all a greedy bunch,
It must be spread more equal, no-one's worth that vast amount,
The time has come for all of them, be prepared to give account.

EF, November 2009.

The Graveyard

In an old graveyard near a country church,
There were headstones straight and leaned,
The newest ones they had family flowers,
The old showed signs where friends had weaned.

The old slate stones were cracked and split,
They had stood for two hundred years,
No more they witnessed family life,
No more a valley of tears.

For the generations all have gone,
And their ghosts have turned to dust,
The surrounds of ornamental rails,
Are corroded up with rust.

There's no-one now concerned for them,
They are greeted with creatures unknown,
Each one with a lovely bunch of flowers,
They are caring for a stone of their own.

Now every year when families meet,
To remember all those who have died,
There are headstones old deserted and bare,
Once encircled with people who cried.

But once it was they adorned the place,
With a statement loud and clear,
They whispered grace to the human race,
"Say a prayer for me down here".

EF, November 2009.

"No Pope Here"

These words I heard some years ago,
From whom they came I do not know,
For scribbled on the bricks with smear,
The words I read were "No Pope Here",
And down below some poet wrote,
The truth I tell, the words I quote,
    "Those who wrote those words
    They wrote them well,
    For the same is written
    On the gates of hell".

Well, I'll be honest, you must admit
That whoever wrote them had some wit,
And I don't care where he stood in the mud
Though it's likely he had Fenian blood,
Yet even so and I'll say it now
No cobwebs clouded his papish brow.

For many times in the life I steer,
I have witnessed written "No Pope Here",
But never once was I inspired
To paint the walls with my desires,
Yet here it was some poet wrote
The truth I tell, the words I quote,
    "Those who wrote those words
    They wrote them well,
    For the same is written
    On the gates of hell".

EF, November 2009.

Neighbours in Death

I have just returned from a funeral,
The death of a neighbouring man,
He was ill for maybe a year or two
That's when all of his troubles began,
But up 'til that he was always well
He enjoyed the best of good health,
He was known all over the countryside
So today, the community knelt.

They gathered to offer the family support
And to extend the shaking of hands,
Just to say how much they were sorry
And to tell them that we understand,
It's a culture that's steeped in tradition
For centuries it starts with "The Wake",
Where people they gather in numbers,
Their respects they're all wanting to make.

Then everyone joins the procession
For a mile they will walk with the hearse,
To accompany the corpse on its journey
Half a day before they disperse.
The priest he performs a great sermon
For the death of a neighbouring soul,
And then to the tune of the angels
They dibble him into the hole.

And all who are standing there watching
Will each in his turn join the queue,
For as sure as the sun it is setting
The soil will be falling on you,
No-one can escape this finale
It will come to us all in the end,
Pray God when were faced with our maker
He will eye us and call us a friend.

EF, 25th November 2009.

The Widower

Every time I think of you, I close my eyes and cry,
Every time I see your face, waving me goodbye,
Shadows come between us, distance separates,
Lonely days and lonely nights, sadness it creates,
Suddenness and emptiness, leaves my soul in pain,
Knowing in my heart I'll never see my love again,
What is going to happen now, I will never know,
Going by this moment I am feeling very low,
All these years together we could never be apart,
Wishing I could stop it all and go back to the start.

Every time I think of you, the flame it fizzles out,
No amount of stoking seems to satisfy the drought,
The fire has just stopped burning, no amount of coal,
Will ever fill the hunger that I feel here in my soul,
For I am lost without you, and there is no desert map,
I am totally isolated, grief has caught me in a trap,
Oh, come to me and tell me an illusion passed my way,
Comfort me, and let me see and make it go away,
I cannot bear to think of this, please God I am so weak,
Can you give her back to me dear Lord, that's all I seek?

Every time I think of you one hundred times a day,
Refusing to believe it all, it drives my head astray,
I cannot even contemplate now being all alone,
You were such a part of me and now I'm on my own,
Someone even told me to forget and let you go,
That time would heal and very soon soften up the blow,
But I am very sorry, cause that's not the way I feel,
Just let me be, set me free and give me time to squeal.

EF, November 2009.

158

Strange Incident 1964

As true as I'm sitting here writing
This incident happened to me,
At twelve I was fond of the fishing
After chores I always was free.

Then off I would run to the river
In a hurry to get to it quick,
To catch little red breasted tiddlers
With a jam pot, a net, and a stick.

No luck, I was growing impatient
Red breasts were as rare as gold,
You'd never have guessed for a moment
This story about to unfold:

For just as I thought about leaving
I spotted this beautiful fish,
Its breast was a red as a robin
To catch it, I only could wish.

I stretched my foot out in the river
To rest on a big shiny stone,
When suddenly from out of the water
Came a hand, it was all skin and bone.

Well, I drew back my foot in sheer terror
And I trembled with fear at the sight,
I was startled and stiffened with panic
And my heart was already in flight.

Then off like a rocket I scrambled
My mother she started to pray,
She said 'twas the angel that guards me
That saved me from drowning that day.

EF, November 2009.

St Mary's Church 1790

Go back in time
You'll always find
A church in Lisnagade,
With verse and rhyme,
St Mary's shrine,
A place where saints are made.

From those days on
The years outshone
A church in Lisnagade,
Where people share,
And readers dare,
And children make the grade.

Two hundred years
Of joy and tears
A church in Lisnagade,
With funerals cold,
And weddings bold,
And family folk are laid.

In years to come
Our bodies numb
A church in Lisnagade,
New people there
Will stop and stare
Live spirits all invade.

With christening robes
And visitor probes
A church in Lisnagade,
Oh, to this day
We go to pray
Beneath the leafy shade.

EF, November 2009.

The Family Kite

This was no ordinary kite, ambitious in size
It was cut up and made up, designed up to rise,
We ordered new linen, we stitched it with care,
We created a border so the thing wouldn't tear.
Then into the middle we stretched it with dowels,
We secured it together down into its bowels,
It was sturdy and strong, yet light for the gales,
A couple of coke cans we attached for the tails
The cord it was ordered, three hundred yard spool,
With names we all christened this kite 'Super Cool'.

Well, bigger than all of us, it stood on our lawn,
We waited for wind from the first crack of dawn,
Then up it went higher, kept reducing in size,
The kite disappearing up into the skies.
With anchors we held the thing down in the ground,
I cannot describe the excitement all round,
The children they said they could hear the kite sing,
Their scribbles on cardboard they sent up the string.
With no-one aware of the change in the breeze,
No-one could predict that the wind it would ease.

Now slowly the flyer it made its way round,
The linen was spinning it was heading for ground,
With three hundred yards of cord on the line,
I knew in that moment I had so little time.
To bring the kite home was my only desire,
When suddenly it caught it the high electric wires,
It wound them together there were sparks in the air,
We scattered in panic, all united in prayer.
But nothing could stop it we were in for a shock,
For the power it was off for a turn of the clock,
To this present day I can remember it still,
From the board of electric, a large repair bill!

EF, November 2009.

Little Boy Dead

It's very hard not to feel angry
At the death of another wee boy,
Horrific, the terrible injuries,
Your mind it would really annoy,
The boy was attacked by a killer,
By a dog called the family pet,
The parents they cover his actions
They'll say he was never a threat.

What planet do these people live on?
They simply have no common sense,
When knowing a dog of this nature
Should be locked up behind a wire fence,
But maybe that's exactly the problem
With people like these on the loose,
For in truth, it's the only conclusion,
They haven't the brains of a goose.

They'll show his wee face in the papers
And splash it all over the news,
The authorities all rushing and queuing
In a panic to give us their views,
No doubt they will fill us with bullshit
And as usual the truth they will hog,
If you'd ask me the fate of the owner,
Well, I wouldn't be shooting the dog.

EF, 1ˢᵗ December 2009, written with anger.

162

A Falling Star

Last night I witnessed a falling star
And it fell from the tail of the plough,
Its plummet to earth was fast and swift
But it's back up there again now.

Well I can say without a doubt
That a star fell out of the plough,
And it hit the ground with out a sound
But it's back up there again now.

Yes I know for sure this falling star
Fell out of the sky from the plough,
It's hard to believe for all of you
For it's back up there again now.

Those brightly shining seven stars
Last night formed up the plough,
'Til one fell off before my eyes
But it's back up there again now.

Last night I witnessed a falling star
Six stars made up the plough,
I don't know when that star returned
But it's back up there again now.

EF, 1ˢᵗ December 2009.

No Return

It always takes a little while
For a man to realise,
That all of his possessions
Will be useless when he dies,
For he cannot take it with him
And his life he can't reverse,
There's no windows in his coffin
And no drawbar on the hearse!

It usually takes a lifetime
For a man to realise,
That he won't be here for ever
No matter what he tries.
Some day the harp will call him
He will have to leave the crowd,
No where for his belongings
No pockets in his shroud.

But sooner, yes, or later
A man will realise,
That the world can live without him
When he's travelling through the skies,
Not a penny will go with him
Not a coin to pay his way,
No assurance 'til he gets there
As to whether he can stay.

So it's better in the present
For a man to realise,
That after just a short time
Everyone will dry their eyes.
Share it round when you are with them
Keeping little when you go,
Make the journey light and easy
Leave the seeds and let them grow.

EF, 3rd December 2009.

To Each His Own

Paddy had a bicycle
Its frame was built for two,
And every day the back of it
Was shared with brother Hugh,
They went to do their shopping
Every morning on the bike,
And when they rode in tandem
They were very business like.

Now Paddy always exercised
The front end of the bike,
And Hugh sat up behind him
When they ventured on a hike,
They covered miles together
With no petrol stops to make,
Hugh reminding Paddy constantly
That he could never overtake.

One evening Hugh was very sick
From a meal the night before,
So Paddy headed out alone
For tablets from the store,
He jumped upon his bicycle
And he cycled into town,
When in the twilight evening
Met the Forces of the Crown.

Well they booked a faulty tail light
It was not working on the back,
They were lacking much in mercy
Well, they were the men in black,
Paddy calmly wiped his forehead
To the policeman he was blunt,
"Hughie always rides that bike sir
As for me I ride up front!".

EF, 4ᵗʰ December 2009.

Life's Sorrows, Life's Joys

There were whispers of joy all round the church
And the Christening was about to begin,
New life was brought for the very first time
To remove all traces of sin,
The mum and the dad, and the grandparents too,
And the brothers and sisters and all,
They came to welcome this brand new life
Wrapped up in a beautiful shawl.

Then back to the house for a family meal
Excitement was flowing like grace,
With everyone calling the baby by name
Put a smile on every ones face.

Now only a mile or two down the road,
There were tears on a different scale
For the sorrow that landed upon their door
Left a family with a desperate tale,
The news came in of their daughter's death,
A young life in her twenties was dead,
Her car had collided with a four by four,
Surely every parents dread.

They gathered around the family home,
No smiles on any ones face,
With every one speaking of her by name
A treasure no-one can replace.

EF, 7ʰ December 2009.

Abuse

Abuse, abuse, abuse, abuse,
On the news now night and morn,
But back in the days when I was at school,
There was abuse, and it was the norm.

For the teachers slapped you every day
For the things you did not know,
And without the stick, the knuckle bone,
Your head would have suffered the blow.

They picked on all the stupid ones
And torture was the daily class,
Out of the frying pan into the fire
When you stood on secondary grass,

For it was equally just as bad
Spare the rod and spoil the child,
That's all the teaching they could do
Their actions were reviled.

They beat their way through Irish class
And geography was the same,
In the PE rooms they beat your arse
Like in some perversive game.

So today we know it happened
When we hear of child abuse,
It was a practiced daily ritual
For which there's no excuse.

EF, 8th December 2009.

Sweetheart

When first we met we used to meet
Outside her own four walls,
And dream of days as man and wife,
My memory now recalls,
All wrapped inside my brown suede coat
We'd kiss and cuddle close,
With arms entwined we'd dwindle time
And wish we could propose.

Well, it was so, our love did grow
We'd often hum and sing,
And save the pennies that we earned
To buy a diamond ring,
We planned the track no turning back
The date we could not wait,
When wedding bells would keep us dwell
Outside our garden gate.

Now summer days and winter days
And autumn days and spring,
Would soon go round and come around
And children they would bring,
And soon like oak trees full of bloom
Their leaves would start to sprout,
For we'd be heading off to bed
When they were going out.

A lifetime passed all in a flash
We'd dream of her four walls,
And how we used to cuddle close
When wind and rain would fall,
But now my journeys empty
I just visit her and weep,
The grave is now her brown suede coat
As she lies beneath my feet.

EF, 10th December 2009.

Grief

There are no words,
Just tears,
Tears that fill up
Your vocal cords,
Expand your Adam's apple,
Speechless,
Your throat thumps,
With grief and sorrow,
Helpless, a watcher on,
Words inadequate,
Sharing the moment
And wanting too,
What's shared is halved
And you want it,
Still no words,
They would only be
In the way,
But silence shares the day.

EF, 11th December 2009.

Seasons Last

Oh the winter is upon us, the weathers turning cold,
It's coming up to Christmas time, snowy days unfold,
Mornings start off frosty, evenings drop in fast,
Darkness cuts the light short and soon the day is past.

Red streaks at night time, stretched across the sky,
Leaving all our senses numbed, our bodies mystified,
For sights like these are rarely seen, Heaven's open door,
Preparing for the new day we've never had before.

The Autumn's work is done now, trees are nude and bare,
Sights behind the branches of a world we now can share,
Hidden for the season by the leaves of green and gold,
Standing with their presence high, so elegant and bold.

Hoping for the Spring time with Winter still to come,
Talking of the Summer time with warmer days begun,
Not a pleasant season, with cold and frost and snow,
A dark and dismal reason not to leave the bungalow.

But sooner than we realise, cracks will split the ice,
Spring around the corner, brings a touch of paradise,
Christmas days and Winter days, end another year,
Days are long and sunny, evenings bright and clear.

The cycle so continues, Winter, Santa, flowers in Spring,
With Summer in the middle and the holidays to bring,
And Autumn leaves are falling, trees are nude and bare,
The Winter it is back again, with cold and frosty airs.

EF, 12th December 2009.

Paula

Such youth and beauty should not die,
In tears of cries and sad goodbyes,
No child should have to bear such pain,
Such youth and beauty should remain,
An earthly world still unexplored,
A child so young and much adored,
Abundant love so much to give,
A future full of life to live.

Such youth and beauty should not die,
So short in years, the questions why,
A poorer world, is Heaven's gain,
Such youth and beauty should remain,
For we can only see what's bright,
Our lives are used to lamp and light,
And darkness we all put on hold,
With no desire, if truth be told.

Such youth and beauty should not die,
And there are no words to justify,
No voice of ours can yet explain,
Such youth and beauty should remain,
The knowledge that she is with God,
Leaves still with us a path to trod,
A long and winding painful track,
No youth, no beauty, coming back.

EF, 16th December 2009.

More than Enough

To say you don't care about money
Is easy when your pockets are full,
With the bank and a cheque book behind you,
Your life it should never be dull.

Affording a gardener 's no problem
You can add a wee bit to your house,
Your car you can change in the morning,
Pay someone to look for that mouse.

You can book a nice holiday in Paris
You can fly round the world on a plane,
With cash hanging out of your pockets,
It's no bother you can't feel the pain.

So that is the problem with money
Some people they couldn't care less,
They've always had plenty to scatter,
From sowing the seeds of success.

It must be a wonderful feeling
To know there is plenty in store,
For no matter how much you misuse it,
There's always loads waiting and more.

Most people do care about money
For there's never enough to go round,
We spend our lives grasping and grabbing
To get that wee smell of a pound.

EF, 17ᵗʰ December 2009.

Guidance in Silence

Listen to the silence when it wallows in your ears,
Pretend you do not hear it, that it soon will disappear,
Ignore the signs of sadness, hoping gut will overcome,
Is to shut out all your feelings, is to play at acting dumb.

It is easy to be stubborn, and to revel in your notions,
But doing this is risky; it can tramp on your emotions,
Playing games is dangerous, trying to act the fool alone,
Listen carefully to the silence, you will not be on your own.

Speaking words are very useful, so important is to hear,
Recognising to the difference, it will overcome your fear,
No person is an island when it comes to flesh and bone,
For it simply is impossible, if your heart is like a stone.

Reach beyond where you are going, stop and do it now,
Listen to the silence, bow your head and make a vow,
Allow yourself the freedom to express, you're just a man,
Strong enough to state it clearly, that in life you need a hand.

There're no roses for the hero, there're no medals for the brave,
With no stopping of the planet, when you're lying in your grave,
There's a world of people round you, only willing for to share,
Listen to the silence daily, appreciate how much they care.

Take a moment of reflection, let the silence fill your ears,
Come to terms with your emotions, satisfy your soul for tears,
Understand your inner feelings, they will guide you on your way,
Give a chance to all Gods creatures they will help you every day.

EF, 18th December 2009.

Broken Hearted

Wednesday the twenty forth,
Today is Christmas 'eve,
Whilst many will be happy
There are many who will grieve,
For time has brought them trouble
There's an empty heart to bear,
A loved one has been taken
There is silence in the air.

No parcel will replace them,
No present take their place,
A word that's kindly spoken
Will never reach their face,
The walls are filled with sadness
The sun has shone its last,
The level of the sadness
Will never seem to pass.

A voice that once brought comfort
And hope to all concerned,
Has left them now forever
And it never can return,
The year has passed so quickly
Yet slowly sure for some,
The bond has been dismantled
For a loved one has succumbed.

And when it comes to Christmas
And to Christ our Saviour's birth,
Take time for those in mourning
For they are left to face the earth.

EF, 24ᵗʰ December 2009.

The Cottage

There's a little cottage sitting by the roadside,
There's a woman living in the old homestead,
There's a river running past the whitewashed gable,
There's a nail tied in the bun behind her head.

There's a roof that's made of thatch hanging over,
There's a chimney smoking soot into the air,
There's a window pane no longer transparent,
There's a door with broken boards a worse the wear.

There's a stove and there's a griddle in the kitchen,
There's a woman in her nineties baking bread,
There's a bag of flour adorning a black raven,
There's a jug of buttermilk with mildewed head.

There's a bag of turf that's sitting by the fireside,
There's a cat that wouldn't even catch a mouse,
There's a hen and there's duck and there's a turkey,
There's an atmosphere of harmony in the house.

There's a broken chair that hasn't rocked in ages,
There's a table sitting on the old hearth floor,
There's a mug as clear as day she is left handed,
There's a teapot black as coal for her to pour.

There's a Tilly lamp that's hanging from the ceiling,
There's a bucket used for water from the well,
There's a way of life that's disappearing swiftly,
There's an end in sight for when she will not dwell.

EF, 28th December 2009.

Practical Beginner

Some people haven't got a clue what to do
When it comes to the practical things,
They never become too involved or resolved
Or concerned with the headaches it brings.

But it's not their fault that they don't exalt
When it comes to the practical things,
For they never were taught,
And they wouldn't purport
To pretend that they know everything.

So all of the while they approach with a smile
When there're practical things to be done,
When it comes to ideas for them to decide
They simply just say they have none.

But it's never too late for the spade and the grape,
Or to drill a big hole in the wall
Is it ever too late for the garden to shape,
Is it ever too early to crawl?

Well, now is the time when you're still in your prime
And there're practical things to be done,
If someone should ask of the talents you have
For God's sake, don't say you have none.

So get on your bike, buy the tools that you like,
And get stuck right into the action,
You may be amazed at the gifts you possess,
A life full of art and attraction.

EF, December 2009.

Your Autumn

Your Autumn poem is beautiful
Of the friend you so fondly knew
And from the way that you have described it
I think that we knew her too.

It just cannot be a coincidence
And it must be the same shocking view,
On the fifteenth day of November
The year two thousand and two.

It was early that terrible morning
We were having our ten o'clock tea,
When out through the pane of the window
A small little plane we could see.

It was flying around all in circles
The tragedy it had yet to unfold,
And nothing could ever prepare us
For the horrible news we were told.

Someone called and said they have found her
A vision was clear from the air,
We simply refused to believe it
Our minds were just saying, "Well Dare".

But truthful it was as you know it,
As the day it progressed became clear,
Since then there's this emptiness feeling
Someone special is no longer here.

EF, December 2009.

The Robin and The Sparrow

There's a robin and a sparrow
Eating crumbs at lightning speed,
It is nice to put the bread out
And to watch them when they feed,
For they never stop a moment
And they constantly observe,
With danger all around them
They stretch out their little nerves.

Well, it only takes a second
They can move from A to B,
In the blinking of an eye
They can light up on a tree,
Then back again in hunger
Fast food the menu serves,
With dangers all around them
They will test their little nerves.

For surely comes the magpie
Less risks prepared to take,
He sits and gases curiously
Looking down his bake,
But in between the stalling
When he darts about and curves,
The sparrows and the robins
They will test their little nerves.

For it's nice to sit and watch them
Eating crumbs at lightning speed,
Darting in and out of danger
In their efforts to succeed,
For it only takes a second
As they twist and turn and swerve,
The sparrows and the robins
They stretch out their little nerves.

EF, December 2009.

The Reservoir

Looking up the silent hill the reservoir is still,
Piped beneath the ground the concrete structure fills,
A fresh supply of water, sparkling, sweet and clean,
Reaches people daily, duly fit for king and queen,
A tap when anti-clockwise turns water gushes out,
Preserved within the reservoir fills the kettle spout,
A tribute to the brave endured a monument create,
Willing hands no longer stand arrive at Heaven's gate.

Remember back to beaten track, shovel, pick, and spade,
Days of graft and hickery shafts when everything was made,
Back in time to dust and grime with barrows full to brim,
A line of men not seen again bred workers all within,
Oh welly boots and boiler suits and clad in duffle coats,
When back in school the little fools were classified as goats,'
Pushing pens don't make amends when dry above the brow,
Debts we owe will have to go to men who gripped the plough.

But time is running out now, the pipes will soon be dry,
The past will be forgotten we will have to say goodbye,
For new is in and old is out, technology paves the way,
The reservoir I'm sad to say is soon to have its day,
Well, that's the news that's floating all about the land,
The year ahead and word will spread, no longer in demand,
They're making it redundant now, it's past the sell-by-date,
The men who push the pens again deciding on its fate.

EF, December 2009.

Day Dreamer

I had this dream and I had it often
And it was always very real,
Every time I closed my eyes
I experienced this ordeal.

This dream began to haunt me
And to captivate my mind,
Sometimes it forced my eyelids
To see them from behind.

And then often I was tempted
To resort myself to bed,
To see if I could find this dream
That was running through my head.

For even during the course of day
I would try and find some sleep,
So daunting was this dream I had
Inside my mind so deep.

But one day this dream it left me
With no answers to provide,
I never could recapture it
No matter how I tried.

And why that is I do not know
'Cause it haunted me for years,
But I wakened up one morning
And this dream had disappeared.

EF, December 2009.

January One 2010

The millennium now is a decade old
Today is two thousand and ten,
If you have failed to make amends
Then start all over again,
The decision now is yours alone
You fail if you do not try,
You can't take back the passing years
But new ways you can apply.

It won't be easy that's for sure
Old habits all die hard,
But try a little, don't give in
And just be on your guard,
It's worth the effort you will see
For your life will start to change,
And for a while you'll even think
That all of it seems strange.

But take a tip from me today,
Stop cursing for a start,
Don't pass on filthy mobile jokes
And have a change of heart,
Your acts will make a difference
To a world that can't abide,
When confronted with your maker
He will know how hard you tried.

EF, 1ˢᵗ January 2010.

Greed, Greed

He bought oul things he'd never need
The stuff that he thought he wanted,
To satisfy all of his wild desires
All the ones inside that ranted,
He took them home and he stored them up
The roof space was congested,
The dust and the mice were eating up
The money he had invested.

He had more oul things he'd never use
And his money was all wasted,
For every time he saw a new toy
He just went out and chased it,
He was buying things for the sake of it
Not a thought for a rainy day,
He would double up on the groceries
And in a week's time throw them away.

And for what? Why all of the panic?
What's the need? It seems such a sin,
Just to store it all up in the roof space
Or to throw it out into the bin,
So take time and reflect on the question
When the urge it comes on you to spend,
Do I need, Do I need, Do I need it?
It's the thought that I'd recommend.

EF, 2nd January 2010.

Happy Birthday Mrs

Another day, another year,
A birthday celebration,
The more of them you seem to have,
The more the acceleration.

They only come but once a year
A birthday appreciation,
You eat and drink with all of them,
The family congregation

Well, everybody comes along
A birthday dedication,
And afterwards you suffer from
An evening's dissipation.

But common sense prevails for now,
A birthday moderation,
Remember getting on in years,
The daily medication.

But three days into January
A birthday reputation,
The years that we all celebrate
There's little lubrication.

So here's to her, my closest one,
A birthday presentation,
To wish you health and happiness
The family combination.

EF, 3rd January 2010.

When You're Smiling

'When you're Smiling,
      When you're Smiling',
Is a very famous song,
The words were found in pockets
On an anonymous vagabond,
Were they written by this man?
Or found and kept intact?
No-one can be certain
Is it false, or is it fact?

'When you're laughing,
      When you're laughing'
Is a very powerful line,
It's as relevant today
As it was back then in time,
For to think when you are laughing
That the sun shines from the sky,
Is a comfort to the writer
If his time had come to die.

For he states it clear when crying
That you just bring on the rain,
Or could he mean your actions
Would be purely just in vain?
But we never will be certain
For this vagabond is dead,
Could the words found in his pocket
Have been etched inside his head?

EF, 4th January 2010.

Serious Sickness Blues

Sickness is an awful thing
And it's awful hard to bear,
It messes up your system
Thinking life is so unfair,
Who's to blame? Is very common
And the urge to say, "Why me?"
It can leave you feeling bitter
In a mode of misery.

And depending on the impact
How severe the illness is,
It can leave you feeling guilty
Like there's nothing more to give,
There's an emptiness in sickness
Like I've never felt before,
And you're constantly concerned
Of what the future has in store.

Will it ever be much better?
Knowing all that's in the past,
Will I 'ere return to normal
Be it slow or be it fast,
You can not retrace your footsteps
All the years of healthy form,
When there never was a problem
Hale and hearty was the norm.

Some days you wake up thinking
You could take the world apart,
But your body soon reminds you
Every time you make a start,
That no longer you're the person
Whom you used to be before,
And you'll never be that person
For your health you can't restore.

So, just make a big decision
Take your life where it is now,
Accept, that God has made the changes
You can't reverse it anyhow. (*EF, 5ᵗʰ January 2010.*)

Make a Contribution

Most people have a working life
And a contribution make,
From early hours to evening late
And for mostly others sake,
Yes some ones going to benefit
From the efforts you afford,
And to make a living working
Brings an honest due reward.

Now you may be a plumber, or a joiner on a site,
Or you could be a doctor, or a nurse that's working nights,
You may even be a road sweep, that wipes the footpaths clean,
You could even be a chimney sweep
Whose days are far from green.
And maybe you're a teacher, trying to pass your skills to more,
Or maybe you're a footballer who's trying to get a score,
There's the butcher and the baker
From the cake they want a slice,
There's the many civil servants who are trying to be nice,
There's are engineers and craftsmen
They all cover people's heads,
And the scores and scores of cleaners
Who are grossly underpaid,
And there are many, many others having work is like a Pill,
With the average daily dosage, exercising all their skills.

Most people have a working life
And a contribution make,
But illness is the hardest work
You could ever undertake,
So be thankful if you're busy
It's the pills of great reward,
Knowing some ones going to profit
From the efforts you afford.

EF, 6th January 2010.

Time Moves On

What we always should remember
Is that time moves on,
And the things that make the headlines
Are tomorrow dead and gone,
When you think of fame and fortune
All the names up there in lights,
There are always brand new faces
Who will captivate the sights,

Think of all the earthly leaders
Who in turn have ruled the world,
Think of all the bloody wars
And the holocausts unfurled,
They in turn have had their glory
But their ghosts are all that's left,
Time forsook them to the shadows
Long forgotten in life's theft.

What we always should remember
Is that time moves on,
What is written up in history
Had a light that clearly shone,
But today it's out of memory
And today it's out of sight,
What was once a blazing icon
Is no longer shining bright.

EF, 7ʰ January 2010.

Deep In Prayer

I deeply pray today Lord
For those who are in need,
I deeply pray today Lord
For those who suffer greed.

I deeply pray today Lord
For those who try to lead,
I deeply pray today Lord
For those the world can't feed.

I deeply pray today Lord
For voices when they plead,
I deeply pray today Lord
For ears that never heed.

I deeply pray today Lord
For those who cannot read,
I deeply pray today Lord
For leaders to succeed.

I deeply pray today Lord
For every worldly creed,
I deeply pray today Lord
For nations, seed and breed.

I deeply pray today Lord
For your good hands to weed,
I deeply pray today Lord
That quickly you proceed.

EF, 11th January 2010.

Good Riddance

By chance it was the other day
They crossed each others paths,
The funeral of a comrade
Closed another paragraph,
For many years had slipped away
And each one had a tale,
Of all that they succeeded in,
And much where they had failed.

And as they shook each others hands
Held firm in a silent grip,
Emotions filled their eyes with tears
To the days of comradeship,
And one, he whispered softly,
As he leaned so frail and fray,
"Do you remember back" to such an' such,
"God them were the good old days".

"Oh indeed I do, I feel like you
I remember them very well,
But when I think back the truth be told
They remind me much of hell",
And he too leaned across to him
His skin was blue and black,
I too recall those good old days
Pray God they never come back.

EF, January 2010.

Politics

Politics yes, or Politics no,
      A decision I must make,
Do I simply stay at home,
      Or go and claim a stake,
I'm entitled to my vote,
      A difference can create,
With stroke of pen a message send,
      My views communicate.

Politics yes, or Politics no,
      But think about it hard,
Your freedom of expression,
      Is dealt into your card,
Take the time to study well,
      Which party tops the poll,
Don't wait until the dark of day,
      To throw away your soul.

Politics yes, or Politics no,
      Too often Orange or Green,
Don't vote for waving colours,
      Or those with voices mean,
Study what they'll do for you,
      And read their message well,
It can only make the difference,
      Paradise or living Hell.

EF, February 2010.

A Bitter Life

Many people end their lives feeling very bitter,
And carry with them all the years an awful lot of litter,
They gather up the baggage and they never let it drop,
Included in their weekly list, every time they shop.

A family chip can sit for years, festering on a shoulder,
A story bold from days of old can just become a boulder,
An argument, no matter what, has never went away,
And now the extra burden is a terrible price to pay.

So life becomes a problem from the emptiness of weight,
And leaves a person shattered, in a very broken state,
Electrified with voltage they simply can't let go,
No matter what you tell them, they do not want to know.

A grievance with a neighbour flogs them all their life,
Over something stupid, causing lots of pain and strife,
They bottle up the takings, won't be first to let it go,
"I'm the one to rule the roost, and I will run the show".

But bitterness is galling and it's awful hard to swallow,
Can leave you with an ending, nothing more than shallow,
And all because of nothing, and all for why? For what?
The person time forgot, when you occupy your plot.

So let it go, spit it out and don't take it to the grave,
For God is watching all of us and how we all behave,
Undo the chains of baggage that keep your life in prison,
Don't find yourself in shackles when your spirit has arisen.

EF, February 2010.

Obedience

I cannot forget those days of old
When youth was on my side,
When running on an errand
For my mother was with pride,
You never stopped to say
"I can't", "I won't", "I will not go",
You jumped on board your bicycle
And you shouted, "Cherrio".

And pushing in your pocket down
As deep as you could frown,
You guarded very carefully
That shining, half a crown,
And in your head repeating
All the things your Ma had said,
The milk, the eggs, the butter
Don't forget the loaf of bread.

"Remember now to watch your change
And bring it home to me,
For I'll need what I can muster up
To meet the coal mans fee",
And I'd be shouting back at her
"Now don't you worry Ma",
For by this time I'd be heading
Round the corner, past McGraths.

For nothing was a problem in those days
When we were lean,
We'd be in and out of town again
As fast as runner beans,
You never knew to argue
And you'd never turn your cheek,
You carried out your duty
Was the language you would speak.

EF, February 2010.

Hospital Visit

Now I suffer from a great lack of patience,
And do you know it's a wonderful thing,
For it exposes your insides to the weather
Agitation and annoyance it brings.

Now because of this great lack of patience
My watch is the most gazed upon,
Every time my wrist visits my eyelids
Another ten minutes have gone.

This appointment I had at three thirty
And now it's away past the hour,
I can't understand what is happening
As my feelings they rapidly turn sour.

Well a lady who is sitting right opposite
Looks at me and we both shake our heads,
Recognition of a stranger in common
It is obvious without a word said.

We both suffer from a great lack of patience
Why is it they are running so late?
My appointment it was for three thirty
A quarter to five's a long wait.

But as a patient I will have to be patient
For there's a risk I will drive myself mad,
Deep breaths and a prayer or two later
At the sound of my name I'll be glad.

EF, February 2010.

Our Family Pet

Sneaking about, noiselessly
Pawing its way around,
Up on the garden table,
On to the wall, not a sound,

Then up onto the pillar
Stuck beside the patio door,
Springing effortlessly
To the roof of the garden store.

Staring down, penetrating
Eyes piercing into your face,
Like a perched panther
Waiting, just to give chase.

All the time in the world
To waste like a mad poacher,
Teeth snarling, white in saliva
Daring you to even approach her.

Her black coat shining like polish
Reflects the sun like a new shoe,
Surrounded by the background,
This image of fur in a sky so blue.

Evening time lurking at the back door
Transformed into this lovely wee pet,
She sits with her mouth wide open
From a failed days haunting,
Our wee cat.

EF, February 2010.

My Mistake Lord

Sometimes I forget what
My first journey should be,
'Cause my head is consumed on a worldly spree,
I awaken with plans
To do this and that,
Sometimes I forget to thank God for my lot.

For I promised myself
I would always take time,
To remember each day that we tread a fine line,
And that nothing is certain,
There is no guarantee,
That tomorrow will come or be trouble free.

So before I retire
To my hopefully sleep,
I just take a wee minute and explore myself deep,
And I turn to my maker
Who remembers me well,
To guard and protect me and come to me dwell.

For day passes day
And the nights all take flight,
You blink with your eyes
And they're all out of sight,
So I'm trying my best
A blind eye to the sod,
But reminding myself
That I walk with my God.

EF, February 2010.

Modern Technology

It used to be I could remember telephone numbers,
I had them stored deep in my brain,
And every time I'd ring someone
I would tune in again and again.
Well I brought them to the surface
With the computer in my head,
There was little effort needed just to waken them from bed.

Then one Christmas all my family
Bought a mobile phone for me,
And everyone insisted it would leave my memory free.
So I transferred all my numbers from my brain to this 'mod con'
Well I know that I had hundreds, and on them relied upon.

Now everything it went so well I had this new found friend,
I only had to touch it and a message it would send,
In fact if I am honest, it was always by my side
Reminding me that part of me it only could provide.

For as the weeks and months went by,
I never searched my brain,
I would simply move my arm, take out my mobile phone again,
And soon my memory cottoned on the numbers were erased,
Each one by one they disappeared I surely was amazed.

I now was so dependant; this phone had lured me in,
I couldn't do without it; I was a sucker to begin,
And sure enough you've guessed it, one day I could have cried,
For with out an explanation my mobile phone, it died.

Well there was I in limbo my memory it was void,
I could not recall the numbers my brain was unemployed,
It was a most expensive lesson; it stung me to the bone,
For I had to start all over again, with a brand new mobile phone.

EF, March 2010.

Spuds or No Spuds

It used to be when we were young
We had to gather spuds,
We did not always like it,
And sometimes the tears would flood,
For it was always very cold
The frost would bite your hands,
We sat on an open trailer
To visit the farmers lands.

The fact that we got off from school
This always was a bonus,
But backache was a killer
There were no rewards for slowness,
For no sooner had the digger dug
And opened up a drill,
'Til he was heading back again
You never could stand still.

But one by one the baskets filled
The boxes in the field,
And often a rich harvest
For the farmer it would yield,
And usually by the end of day
They were shipped into the byre,
The stalks were left to scan the field
Whilst to bed we all retired.

But nowadays the fields are wet
And the machinery is far too big,
They are only making muck
Sliding up and down the rigs,
But that is progress some would say
You don't pick spuds by hand,
The problem is that sometimes though
The spuds stay in the land!

EF, March 2010.

Relations Run Out Quickly

I have but one aunt left now
And I have one uncle too,
In fact they're both related
They are siblings through and through,
They both come from my mother's side
The only ones that's left,
And whilst they are in their eighties
Life still treats them both the best.

Oh I know they have their aches and pains
And they have pills galore to take,
But still it's great to see them both
Alive and wide awake.
Now I would know them both so well
And I would keep in contact too,
I'd lift the phone every now and again
Just to say, "How do you do?".

For their lives are so important still
And it means so much to them,
Just to let them know your thinking
How they're doing every now and then,
For all of us have relations here,
They're a part of who we are,
If you take a little time today
You could lift them to the stars.

Now relations run out quickly
We can soon catch up on them,
As the years of life keep passing
We might never meet again,
I have but one aunt left now
And I have one uncle too,
So I'll try to make sure they know me
As their nephew, through and through.

EF, March 2010.

The married couple

Someday, one of us will die,
It may be quick with no goodbyes,
It may be sudden, warnings not,
It may be swift, an artery clot.

Someday, one of us will die,
It may be slow, time for goodbyes,
It may be long and drawn out,
Maybe prolonged for love devout.

Someday, one of us will die,
It may be fast, a rapid sigh,
It may be slow, from health decline,
But either way it's yours and mine.

Someday, one of us will die,
Makes no difference how we try,
A generation passing through,
And someone else will live for you.

EF, March 2010.

The North

My nervous system shivers
When you speak about 'The North',
And reminisce on tragedies
That time keeps bringing forth.

A river flow of sufferings
Keep running through my veins,
And constantly remind me
More of losses than of gains.

My body feels it's swimming
In an ocean full of tears,
And I can see the bitterness
The hatred and the fears.

The muscles that support me
Grow tight when I recall,
How one side or the other
Loved to watch the other fall.

My bones grow weak with tension
Out of pain for those who died,
And left behind their loved ones
To swim against the tide.

EF, May 2010.

The Seeds of Life

In every good relationship
Nourishment is needed,
Like anything that's growing
You always have to feed it,
Neglect it for a little while
And you will pay the price,
Very soon the atmosphere
Will float about on ice.

Beware when you are thinking
You have made it to the top,
And cannot find the compost
To sprinkle on your crop,
For when you're ripe you're rotting
Dehydrated are your roots,
The buds of life are dying
Screaming out from all the shoots.

So cultivate your friendship
And communicate with skill
For it's sure you will discover
There is much more learning still,
For when you're green you're growing
There is moisture in your heart,
Don't take your love for granted
Make each day a fresh new start.

EF, May 2010.

Fish or Meat?

You could spend your whole life eating fish
Like salmon, plaice and cod,
But there's nothing beats a piece of meat
That's grown on Irish sod.

Now fish live in the water,
And fish live in the sea,
And no-one knows just what they eat
Or where the boggers be.

But cattle eat the green, green grass
That grows beneath your feet
And wander freely in the fields,
Producing healthy meat.

EF, May 2010.

Candle Light

It's amazing how bright
In the middle of the night,
The glow that can come
From a small little light.

It's astonishing, the gleam
In the middle of your dream,
When the fridge door opens
And you're craving for cream.

It's a breathtaking glare
That reaches you there,
When a midnight moon
Makes you stop and stare.

It's a brilliant flame
In a picture frame,
Just to see that fire
Before morning came.

It's amazing how bright
In the middle of the night,
The glow that can come
From a small little light.

EF, May 2010.

Early Morning Madness

Brake lights in the distance,
Longer queues in view,
Sighs of desperation,
And pedals under shoes.

Fighting for the fast lane
And trying to overtake,
Everybody hoping
No-one else will make mistakes.

Ladies on their mobiles
Keeping up to date,
Everybody's rushing
In the hope of not being late.

Bumpers licking bumpers
Pulling out and in,
Changing back and forward
Risking life and limb.

7.30, 7.40, 7.45,
Absolute insanity
Right before my eyes,
Lorries pushing motor cars,
Trailers chasing vans,
accelerators pressing
Hell for leather
Man for man.

EF, May 2010.

Jesus

Jesus, keep your name
Upon my lips
Morning, noon and night.

Stay today
Not far away
And keep me in your sight.

Spare from me
The selfish thoughts
That taint me every day,

And guide me from
Assessments that
Would lead my life astray

EF, May 2010.

Special People

There is someone very special
In every body's life,
A sister, or a husband,
A brother, or a wife,
Should it be a neighbour,
A colleague or a friend,
A father, or a mother,
Who will be there to the end.

And when the load is heavy
And the road it narrows down,
There is always someone special
Who will always be around,
And when the burden deepens
And the weight it bears you down,
It's then that special person
Is always to be found.

So when the futures brighter
And the tunnels full of light,
Don't forget that special person
Keep them always in your sight,
For the road is long and winding
You can always hit a bend,
Don't forget those special people,
You will need them to the end.

EF, 12th June 2010.

(Written for the Relay for Life event, Cancer Research UK.)

Headlines

There's a death,
There's a wake,
There's a funeral,
I call it " your three days of fame",
If your life has been good
Then it's certain,
That the papers
Will not have your name.

It's a time when
The neighbours are helpful,
When family and friends all come good,
You may not have seen them for ages,
but there in your sorrow they stood.

And after the news
It has broken
And the first day it nearly has gone,
They gather first time
In your garden
And stand shaking hands on your lawn.

They flock to your wake
In their hundreds
The second day comes and it goes,
And before you can get your head round it
Three days brings it all to a close.

EF, July 2010.

Caring What People Do Today

Caring what people do today
Is of no concern to me,
How they choose to spend their time
We all would disagree,
For some will spend their time in work
And some won't work at all,
Whilst others shop for hours on end
Around the bargain stalls.

Caring what people do today
Is of no concern to me,
When they rise or go to bed
In sin or trouble free,
For what I think or what I say
Is no concern of theirs,
When choosing where a person goes
Is simply their affairs.

Caring what people do today
Is of no concern to me,
Atheists or Christians,
They are guided conscience free,
No need for me to run around
Or feed them from a dish,
For everyone has got the right
To do what 'ere they wish.

EF, August 2010.

Wedding Day Reflection

They say that a wedding is for a day
But marriage is for life,
With twists and turns along the way,
To test them - man and wife.
Along with joys there's troubles,
With sorrows in between,
But often these can just be rain,
To keep your garden green.

For when you're green you're growing
And there's moisture in your leaves,
But all of this depends upon
What each of you believes.
Just welcome joy with open arms
And wrap them round each other,
And when there's trouble in the air
You'll find that it's no bother.

And during the times of sorrow
When your world just falls apart,
Recall the promises that you made
And embrace them in your hearts.
Spend in love your lives together,
Work and share; kneel and pray;
For all of us support you,
Paul and Susie, here this day.

EF, 19th August 2010.

(Written for my nephew Paul's wedding.)

County Fever September 2010

There's a fever in our county, and it's making people sweat,
For the Cork that's in the battle, is a very dangerous threat,
It has left the people scrambling, many angry and unsure,
For to try and get a ticket is the fevers only cure.

The signs were all a coming, an awakening from the dead,
For sure enough the rising, of the men in black and red,
It has shaken up the interests, of the minds that were at rest,
It has driven up the passions, for these men to do their best.

There are people asking questions, of how long it was before,
There are those who know exactly, it was back in 94'
And similar to the gold rush that set the states on fire,
It has inflamed the hearts of all to bring back Sam Maguire.

There's a longing in the atmosphere, a craving in the air,
An openness for winning, that's included in our prayers,
For every now and then in life, this moment comes along,
When suddenly the euphoria, makes us feel we all belong.

So "Up Down", "Come on Down" from all in county Down,
We urge you and support you to bring back Ireland's crown,
And even those who cannot see their idols in Croke Park
The sight of Sam will satisfy the fevers craving spark.

But we must drink the medicine for the colours not the same,
And be sure the Rebel County will be out to win the game,
But the men in black and yellow will be out to make amends,
When the 19th of September comes, it's the day the fever ends.

EF, 8th September 2010.

(Written for the all Ireland Final Croke Park 19th Sept 2010)

Frank and Aileen

When we first met the pair of you
This is how you were:
Young and free from wrinkles
With lovely shining hair,
We surely miss the times we had
The company that we shared,
But we won't forget the faces
Or the voices that we heard.

25 years later, romance still in the air
It's plain to see that love breaks down,
The years of wear and tear.

We do not meet that often now
Or cross each others paths
But we can't forget the good times
Of all the prayer and laughs,
You two haven't changed a bit.
Well, you know we're telling lies
Fact is you look much better
And with that we'll say goodbye.

25 years later, romance still in the air
It's plain to see that love breaks down
Those years of wear and tear.

With Love -- Eugene & Winifred.

The Locks

At Campbell's Locks where the water falls
On a beautiful moonlit morn,
I stood in prayer in the frosty air
At the start of a brand new dawn.

A train went thundering down the line
And I heard the rooster crow,
The canal reflected morning stars
As I watched the currents flow.

There's little ducks and there's bigger ducks
And there's swans as white as snow,
How each of them survive the cold
I simply do not know.

The sound of a giant jumbo jet
It echoes overhead,
The trails that lie behind it, sure
From powerful engines shed.

And standing there on the granite bare
Where the test of time proves still,
In the peace and calm of the morning sky
My thoughts and worries spill.

I lift my hat to those who toiled
Two hundred years ago,
And toast the froth at Campbell's locks
As I watch the waters flow.

EF, December 2010.

Loneliness

Loneliness is like a belt
Tied tight around your waist
It grips you like a girdle
Strangled up and laced,
It feels like suffocation
Stretched up on your toes,
Your insides like a boxers guts
absorbing thumps and blows.

Loneliness is like a strap
That's cramped around your chest,
It chains your lungs from breathing
Like a cardiac arrest,
It feels like asphyxiation
Your throat is stuffed and dry,
There's feeling of depression
And your soul just wants to cry.

Loneliness is like a band
That's forged around your head,
It blocks your brain from thinking
And leaves your thoughts in shreds,
It feels like strangulation
Your whole body's in a knot,
You simply feel like screaming
Does anyone care or not.

EF, December 2010.

Towpath Snow

There're big paws and there're little paws
and there're paws as large as bears,
There're big feet and there're little feet
on the towpath shedding cares,
There're big leaves and there're little leaves
and there're leaves in the morning sky,
There're big sounds and there're little sounds
of vehicles passing by.

Well right beside the towpath,
the Canal flows everyday,
It started off in Carlingford
on its journey to Lough Neagh,
This time of year it freezes up
the pace it slows right down,
When walking near beside it
it never makes a sound.

But underneath the ice and snow
the currents rush with ease,
The water hens just scurry round
in the early morning breeze,
There's cool and calm around us
and the trees are bare and lean,
The ducks and swans are out of sight
they're nowhere to be seen.

EF, December 2010.

Jo: A Senseless Murder

Oh, what it does to your insides
to the blood that flows in your veins,
To the hair that crawls
on the back of your neck,
And the thoughts
that rampage your brains.

Oh, what it does to your insides
to the feelings that fill you with grief,
To the shivers that endlessly
crowd up your spine,
And swell you with shear disbelief.

Oh, what it does to your insides
to emotions you normally control,
To eyes that are good
at fighting back tears,
To the spirits that govern your soul.

Oh, what it does to your insides
to a faith so embedded in rock,
Oh to the sobbing
and the screams of despair,
A reflection on one of your flock.

EF, 31st December 2010.

Grab All

Throughout his life he always rushed
Like hell to see it through,
That's why he always talked about
The way his life had flew.
The unexperienced moments,
The minutes under pressure,
The hours, the days, the weeks and months
With little time for pleasure.

A goal achieved. Ambition sought
His journey nearly over,
Accumulating earthly things
The comprehensive drover,
A race in time, a light in space,
No star is out of sight,
The driving force within him
Was working day and night.

Throughout his life he always played
His hand with odds against.
He said it was a challenge
When his back was to the fence.
He loved the buzz of business blues
It drove his heart and soul,
But now he finds he's all alone
To face the empty hole. E.F. January 2011.

Make A New Start, 2011

When I sleep in my bed on my pillow at night,
With the sorrows and joys of the day out of sight,
I recall in my dreams the desires of my heart,
For to wake in the morning and make a new start.

The dawn has me changing, but the future is bleak,
For the spirit is willing, but the flesh it is weak.
And those heartily desires, they are only but dreams
Are all lost in the sunshine of daybreak it seems.

But then for a moment there is hope in my soul,
I believe there is reason to achieve such a goal.
So with nothing to loose while ambitions remain,
I will aim for the sky and try over again.

I will tackle the waves and weather the storm,
The miracle of change I will need to perform.
Determined and willing, are strengths I will need,
To shake my bad habits, is the course to succeed.

And there're times I will rise, and yes, I will fall,
There will also be times when I won't try at all.
And during those times when my efforts all fail,
I will pick up the oars and let fly the sail.

For what is my life without stopping and starts?
What is achieved without following your heart?
You shove and you push and raise the bar higher
What makes it worth living
Is that God loves A Trier! E.F. January 2011.

Kernan Lough

Flooding memories I unblock
of my time at Kernan Lough,
Where my mother used to take us long ago,
On a Sunday we young teens.
We would push the prams of wee'uns,
The spring of water helped us all to grow.

We had sandwiches and biscuits and a great big flask of tea,
The rewards for all the walking and the sense of being free,
I remember well the big white swans with their beaks of sunset orange,
They would float upon the water hoping we would share the spoils.

There were people there from Laurencetown
from the village on the Bann,
There were people there from Gilford
all to seek the summer tan,
It was like being at Tyrella Beach
though it wasn't half as grand,
But sure we were none the wiser
at the sea without the sand..

Socks and shoes were all discarded to the pram between the wheels,
In the coolness of the water we would wash out toes and heels,
And for hours we'd sit and paddle well into the afternoon,
Sure the thoughts of Monday morning they would all appear too soon.

Then we'd gather up the dummies
and the bottles and the crumbs,
Now make sure there's nothing missing
was the order from our mum,
Then up the hills and down the hills
the pace was sometimes slow,
The evening sun would shine on us
and our faces all would glow.

By now we're all exhausted, when we reach the Blue Road hill,
We've still a hundred yards to go in the early evening chill,
And the pace got even slower and our little feet were sore,
By the time we reached the garden gate
Our wee legs could walk no more.

Now my heart is full of memories
They're still solid as a rock
Of the days when Mammy walked us
Round the road to Kernan Lough.
Those days linger in my memory
And the years they still unlock
Pushing prams and babies' bottles
Round the road to Kernan Lough.

February 2011.

The Older I Get
The Wiser My Father Becomes...

When I was young and full of life and sometimes easily led,
I never always listened to these words my father said,
"Don't ram headlong into life, take time reduce your speed,
Reflect and learn the difference, what is need and what is greed."

"When everybody's running son
take your time and walk!
Study all the things you say
and think before you talk!
Wisdom costs you nothing lad
but it can pave the way.
Patience is a virtue.
and tomorrow's another day!"

But wisdom is too old for youth my father's words were stale,
Discernment is too big a breath for a young man to inhale,
It's not until the day arrives, when I <u>sit</u> down for a rest
I realise that father's words fall heavy on my chest.

It's now I'm getting older
that I know what wisdom is,
It's now I'm getting wiser
that I hear those words of his,
For as everyday it passes
the recovery time gets slower,
I reap the seeds of wisdom
From the wisdom of the sower.

Eugene Fullerton To The Memory Of My Father

March 2011

Youthful Stories.

Stories could be written
of the days when I was young,
There was always an abundance,
they would roll off peoples tongues,
Old folks could scan the cobwebs
and come up with something new,
The yarns were spit out plentiful
from tobacco they would chew.

We got going to the threshers,
though our mothers weren't so keen,
They could always see the dangers
that our fathers never seen,
We could sit up on the tractors
high up on the bales of hay,
And we never felt the boredom
Young ones say they feel today.

Well, my father worked with horses
they were used to pull the plough,
He would always let me harness
saying no time beats the "now",
Youthful days and youthful stories
precious memories I recall,
If I could live another lifetime
I could not revive them all.

March 2011-03-17

Discover your Inners

Lord, spare me the burdens of anger,
the feeling that lingers in strength,
The notions of justification
that ponder my memory at length.

Lord, give me the power of forgiveness,
the feeling that's weaker than most,
Restricting the way of temptation
the route that allows me to boast.

Lord, save me from grief and from sadness,
the feelings of woebegone days,
From pathetic and poignant lamenting
and from doleful low spirited ways.

Lord, allow me to look for contentment,
the feeling of blissful delight,
Provide me with joy and elation
a glimmer of hope in your sight.

Lord, make me aware of my feelings
to know what is right or is not,
Spontaneous inner reactions
remind me of all I have got.

March 2011